Transforming
the
Corporation

Running a Successful Business
in the 21st Century

Andreas C. Kramvis

Mark from
Andreas Kramvis

Acknowledgements

This book captures learning and conclusions reached over many years and put to practice in multiple, real situations. As such, it is not possible to thank all who have contributed to its genesis. Although the responsibility for the content is solely mine, I would like to acknowledge a few key individuals who have provided comments and others who assisted in its preparation for publication.

First, I would like to thank a number of colleagues for reading the manuscript: Kate Adams, Dave Anderson, Rhonda Germany, Murray Grainger, Ken Gayer and Mike Bennett. Their suggestions were very pertinent. In particular I would like to thank Dave Cote, Chairman & CEO of Honeywell for comments and for providing the introduction.

I would like to thank Tom Buckmaster of Honeywell and Wes Neff of the Leigh Bureau for providing suggestions and guidance to make the content more accessible. I would also like to acknowledge a number of people who have assisted in its editing and publication including Mary Beth Spann, Robyn Squire, Thomas Quartararo and Rich Guastella.

This book would never have been started without the persistent encouragement of my friend Nelson Taxel over many years. He also read and commented on early drafts, as did Agni and Sotos Jacovides. Finally, I would like to thank my wife Shirley for reviewing the manuscript at its various stages and for her constant support for the project.

Contents

Foreword

by Honeywell CEO Dave Cote

The Honeywell story is one of cultural change and renewal. When you go back just nine years, Honeywell had multiple cultures, no coordination, weak earnings, no cash flow, little geographic presence, no company direction, a miniscule new product pipeline, a horrible acquisition history, and several years of massive write-offs. Most companies, analysts, and investors had little faith that we'd ever be more than a lackluster performer.

That's changed. Today, our balance sheet is significantly stronger and our earnings quality is superb, with cash conversion consistently above 100%. We have Great Positions in Good Industries, which gives us the opportunity to gain share in industries that are growing well. One Honeywell has brought us together as a single company that performs. Our Five Initiatives – Growth, Productivity, Cash, People, all supported by our Enablers – give us focus and direction, and our 12 Behaviors help define a global mindset for all of our employees. Our big process initiatives (our Enablers) – Velocity Product Development™, the Honeywell Operating System, and Functional Transformation – are helping us bring the products customers want to market faster and streamline our manufacturing processes and internal support services. Our geographic expansion gets better and better, with about 50% of our sales outside the U.S.

To put our remarkable performance in context, it's important to understand some of Honeywell's history. We started out a decade ago as three companies: legacy Allied Signal, legacy Honeywell, and just as those two companies closed their merger, they announced the acquisition of a third company called Pittway. Almost immediately after the three companies came together, there were earnings misses. The stock price fell by about 50% just as the first recession of the decade began. The company was almost sold to United Technologies, then almost immediately to General Electric (GE). The GE sale fell through in a spectacular fashion. A retired CEO was brought back for one year. September 11th happened. And, five months later, in February 2002, we began.

On arrival, it was clear that turning things around would require a substantial shift in the way we thought about Honeywell. We focused on three areas: having Great Positions in Good Industries, One Honeywell, and establishing our Five Initiatives.

The first area was our portfolio. We had some good businesses, but we wanted to pursue a unifying positioning we call Great Positions in Good Industries – a simple, yet powerful concept, based on the idea that a great position allows you to gain share because you have critical mass in R&D, feet-on-the-street, and in the back office, and a good industry provides a tailwind for growth. Next, we embarked on an effort that we call One Honeywell. Now, you can tell by how sexy that slogan is that we didn't waste a lot of time thinking about what to call it. Although the name may not be exciting, the One Honeywell concept has worked. It's done a lot to transform our company. There is, after all, only one stock price. And, there is no substitute for the "glue" that makes people want to work together – across businesses, functions, and countries. We outlined the Five Initiatives – Growth, Productivity, Cash, People, and our Enablers, things that would help those first four happen. Again, they're not earth-shattering, but they are crystal-clear, basic, and consistently implemented over time. The Five Initiatives help get everybody focused on the same things, doing the right work, and thinking and acting like one single company.

Everybody gets energized by growth, the idea that you are going to get bigger, you're going to do new things, you're going to do stuff that's exciting. We concentrated on four areas – doing a great job for the customer every day; sales and marketing excellence; globalization; and new products and services. Focusing on these ideas is making a big difference for us, and maintaining that focus has helped us outperform our peers, even during the worst recession in 80 years. And, thanks to our disciplined, proven acquisition process, today Great Positions in Good Industries is a reality, not just an aspiration.

When it comes to productivity versus growth, it's important to note that it's not an either/or kind of thing. Growth and productivity go hand in hand. As you grow, you become more productive; and as you become more productive, you grow.

Keeping an eye on our cash performance is critically important, because cash gives us the freedom to invest in the future. Thanks to our focus on this crucial metric, we've gone from free cash flow conversion of about 70% of net income in the last decade to greater than 120% cash conversion in this decade … a huge difference.

Finally, as part of the People initiative, we identified the 12 Behaviors we wanted employees to emulate, and created the Honeywell Performance and Development system to ensure that everyone gets evaluated on the same criteria. We also tied salary planning into the review process, and encouraged differentiated rewards based on performance.

The trick is, however, to always be doing all of these things. It's never just one thing. It's always about people AND process. You need the best people, organized the right way and motivated, plus you need an effective process to pull them together to make things happen. Business Decision Week, a process Andreas created, does this very well.

Business Decision Week pulls all of these critical things together and gets people focused on getting and working with the facts, making decisions, and getting things done. Andreas has done a terrific job of creating and implementing Business Decision Week so it makes things happen in a fact-based way, all focused on bringing together Great Positions in Good Industries, One Honeywell, and the Five Initiatives.

Business Decision Week has been implemented successfully in every business he has run, and has been adopted through most of our Honeywell businesses … not because it was mandated (it wasn't), but because it works.

I've seen Andreas and his team deploy their transformation toolkits – and particularly their Business Decision Week rigor – across a range of end markets, business models, and geographies. It works for them for the same reason our Five Initiatives and 12 Behaviors work as a corporate superstructure – people know what's expected of them and how they will be appraised. As you drive ambiguity out of a complex organization you operate faster and more effectively. Andreas's teams and businesses excel because they know what to expect from their leader and what is expected from them.

The perspective you'll find in this book provides some proven tools that helped one of Honeywell's most talented and seasoned leaders work within our complex global operating environment to help Honeywell achieve these remarkable results.

I heartily recommend this book to anyone who just wants to make things happen with less talk and a lot more action.

—Dave Cote
Chairman and CEO Honeywell

Introduction

The tough recession that began in 2008 put many companies in urgent need of transformation. Suddenly a lot of factors changed and new approaches and strategies are now needed to prosper. This situation also provided me with the final impetus to write this book.

Success in business depends on continuous adaptation. Some companies understand this very well and continuously transform themselves. Others become overtaken by events and, without foreseeing it, arrive at difficult positions where options are limited. In fact, the main option they have open is to transform themselves under the pressure of time and in the absence of additional resources. The recession has multiplied the number of companies which need a new direction and a major transformation.

When I set out on my career I did not set out to develop a methodology to transform companies. However, I have always been extremely curious and never afraid to try new ideas out. Of course, sometimes you have to as continuing to do what you are doing will lead only to a brick wall. I learned this lesson very well when, at age 26, I landed my first job as general manager of a company with 400 people.

However, on accepting the position, I had not fully realized that the reason I won the appointment was that nobody else wanted it because the business was about to go bankrupt. Clear thinking, innovation, persistence and a couple of lucky breaks proved sufficient to enable us to turn the corner and get out of our predicament! In fact, in time, we became very successful.

Over the next two decades I ran other businesses, some headquartered in the United States and others located in Europe. I always sought situations requiring innovation in approach and new concepts. I was involved in selecting and establishing start-up companies in the computer memory field. Then, I joined Pittway, a remarkable Company, not because of its initial size but because of what it achieved. We grew consistently by 25% a year and we established ourselves as the global leader in security and fire systems. I led the international expansion in the security business establishing leadership positions in key markets around the globe. Honeywell purchased the business for over $2.2 billion in 2000.

Over time, I became aware that my willingness to seek projects and solutions that required an innovative approach provided me with a unique framework for how to successfully manage and grow a business. Of course, in and of itself, a business framework is but an abstract ideology. For a business framework to have relevance, it must prove itself effective within the day-to-day operation of the business itself. For a framework to be considered successful, it must be able to withstand the most stressful of conditions and still prove valuable.

In 2002 Dave Cote, the new CEO of Honeywell, presented me with a great test bed for my framework. Honeywell itself was in a bad shape following the merger between Allied Signal, Honeywell and then Pittway and also an abortive takeover by GE. Environmental and Combustion Controls (ECC), home of the iconic round thermostat (with over 8000 people, a global presence and sales over $1.3 billion) had been on a path of long term decline and the downward spiral was accelerating. Over the previous five years, four company presidents had come and gone, but the decline worsened with each passing president and each passing year. This business was in an industry I had not worked in before and, frankly, knew nothing about.

I decided to take on the challenge, cognizant that, if four guys could not save this sinking ship, the likelihood of the fifth one coming to its rescue was not that strong. However, I was curious and could not pass up the opportunity to focus myself, as well as the novel management ideas I had been formulating, into this business in crisis. I knew this situation would put my ideas to the test and so I could refine and further define them.

So I occupied the corner office as the fifth president of the company in as many years—a point not missed on employees and management who were busy marking time and writing resumes.

Within a few weeks of being in the job I decided the business could be improved radically. In fact, I felt certain that, with the correct framework in place and by following a carefully choreographed sequence of action steps, we would be out of the woods within two years. This realization excited me greatly, but what thrilled me even more was my awareness that this impressive business rescue and transformation could be accomplished with our existing investment and funding levels. In other words, we could transform this business with the resources we already had available at the time.

Within three months, the resume writing began to abate and employees started to believe that there could be a way forward. Within 18 months it was clear to key customers that something major was afoot. By the end of the second year, we were in strong stride, accelerating farther every quarter.

By year four, we were in a situation of fully sustainable competitive advantage; we were routinely capturing markets and creating new markets with strong profitability. I left the business after completing almost 6 years as the leader. In a spectacular reversal a business which was spiraling down before 2002, grew sales at a compound rate of 15% and profitability by 24%; return on assets employed increased by 1000 basis points. Since I left, the business has maintained the framework under new leadership and growth is continuing apace.

I started writing this book initially as personal notes I could reuse on future occasions. In the process, I realized I had developed and implemented an intelligent, holistic approach to business transformation that was not mechanistic, but flexible and widely applicable. In other words, as I crystallized my ideas in writing, I realized that the approach I had developed was applicable to many, if not all, businesses needing transformation.

In addition, writing things down provided me the discipline I needed to formalize my approach and reduce it to steps I could easily explain so other people could implement the ideas as well.

I find it fascinating that, as I discussed the approach with colleagues I have worked with for a long time (and they have been through the program described in this book), each of them is aware of particular facets of the framework, but not one got the total picture. I guess only the orchestra conductor is privy to the total score. My desire to help my immediate business colleagues become aware of the gestalt of the framework and processes we all operated within gave me one more reason to convert my notes to a book. However, as I said at the opening, the recession really closed the deal for me!

In 2008, I became President and CEO of Honeywell Specialty Materials, a $5 billion business. This offered the opportunity to test the framework in yet another global business, in yet another industry that was again totally unknown to me. Again this was a terrific test bed. Besides Specialty Materials being diametrically opposite to ECC in terms of their routes to market, assets, capital intensity, products, technology and business models, it also offered the opportunity to test the framework in a great recession!

As the recession was raging out there our progress and margin improvements left many in total disbelief. With the framework firmly established in advance, I was able to help the business grow and create value at lightning speed. We grew our margins through the recession and as the economy began to recover our growth pace accelerated. By 2011 we achieved margins 600 basis points above pre-recession levels and at the very top of comparable companies.

And, with the help of this book, you can too.

What To Expect From This Book

First, the book sets out ideas and a methodology to change a business in a fundamental and holistic way. The objective is to bring the business to the position of being an effective competitor that delivers consistently strong profit growth. This means that over time, everything will improve from the effectiveness in the marketplace, to the efficiency of internal operations, to the way management runs the business and the way employees think about the business.

Although this book is ultimately about strategy and tactics, it was born and has been tested and proven successful in the field. Its foundation is the reality of how you make things happen within available resources as well as how you produce results and create value in the real world.

This is not the approach that will be adopted by the executive who employs a strategy team to tell him what to do and regards his job as that of carrying out the recommendation. This is the approach of a confident executive who is able to:

- Select strategy

- Direct execution

- Recognize the key issues

- Make necessary trade-offs

- Deploy resources at appropriate junctures

The book will help you to sharpen skills and enhance your capabilities in all these areas and more.

The book also focuses on identifying achievement–oriented options. A lot of initiatives and a lot of activities go into achieving results. In most situations, the available options are numerous although the correct ones are few. In other situations (like when a company has lost competitive advantage or financial strength), the set of correct options is even more limited.

What you will read is how to identify and select the right options to obtain strong results. The book sets out the ideas and methodologies to bootstrap a company and progressively put it on a strong footing and on a sound path. Essentially, this book reveals the steps you need to take to create value in a consistent way by employing a carefully crafted sequence of activities. The approach advocates balanced risks and optimizes the probability of success.

The book sets out considerations that have to be taken into account to construct a transformation program. I realize that no two situations are the same, yet I want you to rest assured that the general principles you are about to read can be tailored to your individual situation. They are also applicable irrespective of company size.

I structured the material so that it introduces and explains each aspect of constructing the transformation program, while also instructing you on how to best select each activity and the steps needed to implement it successfully.

A transformation program is time-dependent and involves core capability development. That's why each chapter of the book contains strong ideas that will improve results in the short term and build core capabilities for the long-term.

Each chapter is preceded by a short, real life scenario, under the heading "Chapter in Context". This is to bring to life the content of the chapter. Further each chapter contains both an outline and a summary of the main points for easy reference. However, a transformation program is a multifaceted activity with many moving parts; a robust transformation program can only be achieved when a number of these parts come together in the right way. Although I believe you will find each individual chapter interesting and informative, I strongly advise you to read the whole book so that you will have at your fingertips all the necessary elements for executing a strong transformation program.

For ease of explanation and to develop the framework more solidly, this is how the book unfolds by chapter:

CHAPTER 1
Growth Cost and Free Levers
This chapter discusses how to set up financial targets and explains their limitations in running a business. It addresses issues of cost and what you get for it and it introduces the "free" toolkit consisting of leverage points that can be used to greatly enhance performance for no extra cost.

CHAPTER 2
Mr. New Competes with Mr. Longstanding
Here you will discover what you should look for if you step into a new situation with the goal or expectation of transforming a business you are totally unfamiliar with. It sets some key areas to look for and how to "diagnose" what you are dealing with. These pointers are useful as well for all managers who are longstanding in their positions.

CHAPTER 3
The Role of Management Philosophy
This chapter addresses the importance of having a management philosophy and shows how this philosophy guides action. You will want to pay attention here as without a definite management philosophy it is not recommended you enter into an unfamiliar business as the chances of success are low.

CHAPTER 4
Business Decision Week
In this chapter you will explore how to set up and run an effective operating mechanism for transformation and how you use it to effect change. You can look at the operating mechanism as the major forum where all the transformation activity gets initiated and directed.

CHAPTER 5

Enhanced Decision Making

Here you will learn nine requirements for using practical means to enhance decision-making at all levels in an organization. Enhanced decision-making offers huge leverage and is a cornerstone to success.

CHAPTER 6

Seven Effective Strategies to Produce Results

This chapter continues the theme of free tools first mentioned in Chapter 1. It sets out seven effective strategies for producing great results in the transformation journey.

CHAPTER 7

Risk Balancing and Inside Out Sequencing

Here we talk about risk, how to assess it and how to avoid major pitfalls. This chapter sets out a generic strategy on how to reduce risk in a transformation so as to enhance the probability of strong results.

CHAPTER 8

Finding the Game-Changing Moves

This chapter tackles the issue of identifying big game-changing moves for a business. I define these moves as long-term initiatives that offer substantial competitive advantage. The chapter explains how to identify them and how to implement them.

CHAPTER 9

Synthesizing a Plan to Enable Transformation

Here you will learn how an effective transformational plan goes beyond normal planning as it provides a framework of identifying new classes of activity (which, in turn, enable the transformation itself). You will also learn how to systematically include transformational plans in your annual plans.

CHAPTER 10

Seven Requirements for Effective Change

Here you'll find a discussion of the seven requirements for effective change-management. These will enable you to institute and manage change for success.

CHAPTER 11

Sustainability and Continuous Transformation

This chapter discusses sustainability and how to maintain the competitive advantage created by the transformation effort.

Clearly, this book has not come about because of abstract thinking in a vacuum. Everything in it is the result of practical application and has been tried and tested. There is no hypothesis or conjecture herein but a well-tested methodology. And while my transformational methodology is not the sole one in existence, it is most certainly proven and powerful.

If you decide to embark on a transformation program, be cognizant you are committing yourself to a multi-year effort designed to garner your business enormous results and continuous improvement. While the urgency of starting transformational activity is high if your company is in a situation of stress, I believe the motivation to start should be equally high if you are doing well. From either starting point, if you follow the tenets set forth in this book, you can expect great things.

Transformation Framework: Quick Reference Guide

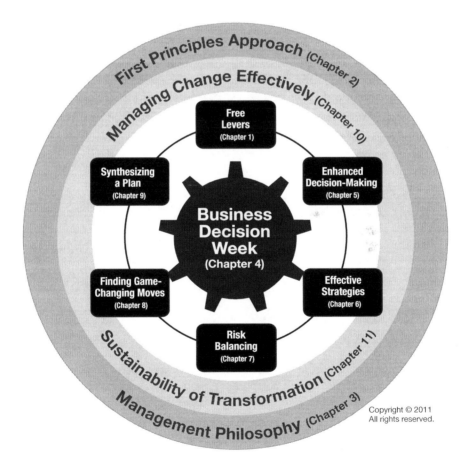

The model above is a visual guide of how the different chapters fit together to provide a coherent framework for transformation.

Looking at the Floor

• • • • •

In August 2002, after two weeks into my job as president of Honeywell's Environmental and Combustion Controls business in Minneapolis, I invited a random selection of middle managers for a discussion over lunch.

When I entered the room, everybody avoided my eyes, and they each sank lower in their seats. I said a few words about myself and my background, and then I invited them to introduce themselves. As you can imagine, the responses were stilted at best.

Then I took the conversation to a more interesting place: What do they do? How do they think things are going? What is their advice to me as a new guy in the business?

Nobody wanted to speak; nobody dared to take the initiative. They just kept staring at the floor. After 30 minutes of what was essentially a monologue, I called it a day.

After the meeting, I remarked to my assistant, "Wow, this is some dynamic group of people you selected for me. They just looked at the floor."

"What do you expect?" she replied. "They are keeping their heads down just in case they get chopped off. We have had constant RIFs (reductions in force) here."

"Thank you," I said. "Now, I really get what's happening."

Soon afterwards, the business leader for our home controls business approached me to have a discussion. He is a savvy consumer marketing hand whose back was against the wall.

"Look," he said, "the competition has great displays with better functionality. Look at our electronic offerings – they are hardly useable. We are only good at electromechanical products. I do not know how long I can keep us in the trade."

When I looked in detail at the products the business leader was talking about, I knew he was right. Our days were numbered. Our only hope was that the competition didn't really have their acts together because we were in danger of being marginalized very fast. Needless to say, this wasn't the best spot for a new boss to be in!

Every August, we put together our annual operating plan. That August, as the management team got together, the sales projections were grim.

Our chief technology officer (CTO), had previously worked in Honeywell's Aerospace business, and he knew his way around electronics. He was blunt.

"Guys," the CTO said, "the pipeline is empty. I will need to hire people with some new skills to design the products you need."

At that point, everybody looked at each other. There was no money. The best idea the management team could come up with? Another round of layoffs. But the problem with layoffs was they were seemingly needed just to make ends meet. How we could fund all the new technical people we required?

After the discussion went back and forth, I said, "Guys, it is simple. Go recruit the people you need, and do it fast! We will need to find a new path forward for this business that is sustainable. Like you, I do not see the total solution today, but we need to move at speed to get new products now."

Our chief financial officer looked grim. "What do I put in for our annual plan?" he asked.

"Put in some good double-digit profit growth numbers and recognize we have lots of gaps," I said. "We will find a way to make the numbers! In any case, it is my neck on the line."

Over the next weeks, months and years, we developed the strategy, put the right people in place and executed our plan. Between 2003 and 2007, we delivered compound sales growth of 15 percent, and compound profit growth of 24 percent. Instead of yet more layoffs, there were plenty of new positions created.

This was a journey of discovery and overwhelming success by a team that learned how to seize the day. It is also a testament of how Honeywell, a large corporation, could provide the framework for this to happen.

Let's focus on the principles that can transform your organization from one that can only think about cutting costs into one that knows how to generate growth and obtain leverage for free.

CHAPTER **1**

Growth, Cost and Free Levers

Chapter Overview

The chapter starts by exploring a few simple financial relationships and how they can combine to produce results. However, if these relationships become the sole means of running a company, they quickly lead to negative results. Confusing financial results with the levers that produce such results is a common shortcoming. The chapter gives examples of a number of the types of levers which exist to transform a company. These levers do not add to cost but they are most commonly ignored; they make the difference between a successful and an unsuccessful company.

Targets and Growth

Target setting is one area which attracts a lot of discussion. Companies often approach it by first picking the kind of results they wish to obtain and then deploying targets within the business that arithmetically add up to the required results. Although this approach can be a starting point for guidance, it is not the optimal method for robust target setting.

In practice a better starting point is to find out the growth rate of the market you are in. The growth rate is important, because if you look at simple arithmetic, sales have the highest leverage on the profit number. Shareholders naturally like to see profits increasing; in most situations if you can produce over a long period of time double-digit earnings growth (e.g., 12-15% annually), you will satisfy requirements (although there is clearly no limit to how high the growth can be). The table on the following page sets out the performance of a company in Year 1 and then four alternative performances or cases for Year 2.

The story these numbers tell is very informative. We have a company which in Year 1 achieved sales of $100. The company is in a market that grows 3% a year on average. (This number may sound low but most companies grow with the Gross Domestic Product [GDP], which in the

(in dollars unless noted)	YEAR 1 Base	YEAR 2			
		Case 1	Case 2	Case 3	Case 4
Market growth (%)		3%	3%	3%	3%
Growth above market (%)		0%	3%	3%	0%
Price		0	0	0	(2)
Sales	100	103	106	106	101
Variable cost	40	41	42	41	41
Variable margin	60	62	64	65	60
Variable margin (%)	*60%*	*60%*	*60%*	*61%*	*59%*
Fixed Costs	40	41	41	41	41
Operating Income (OI)	20	21	22	23	19
OI Growth (%)		*3%*	*12%*	*17%*	*(7%)*

United States, has been about 3%.) If this company grows with the market then sales in Year 2 will go to $103. If all costs grow in line also, all the costs scale up and increase by the same percentage. So in Case 1 the company only produces a profit increase of 3%. This is too low to be acceptable to shareholders.

In the next column, Case 2, the same company has managed to grow by 3% above the market rate for a total 6% growth. Although variable costs have grown in line with volume (the variable margin is staying constant at 60%), the company has managed to keep its fixed costs at the 3% growth level as it did in Case 1. This delivers 12% growth in operating income. Now this performance (if maintained in the long term) begins to be acceptable to shareholders.

In Case 3, the company has managed, in addition to the 6% growth in sales and the limit of 3% in fixed cost increase, to reduce its variable costs (variable margin is now higher at 61%). This produces a 17% growth in operating income, which is a strong result.

Case 4 is really in trouble. It is growing with the market in volume by 3% but it is experiencing a price decrease of 2%; so the sales line is only growing at 1% per year. However, its costs are rising in line with the costs in Case 1. In particular as it is selling the same number of units as the company in Case 1 its variable cost is identical at $41. All of a sudden these factors combine to produce a hefty profits decrease of 7%. Not a healthy position and it did not take much to get there!

It is worth bearing these simple relationships in mind throughout this chapter and indeed the book, as ultimately, transforming a company, is about getting it to the point of delivering steady, reliable earnings growth.

Obtaining double-digit earnings growth is relatively simple in a high-growth market, a situation which presupposes that your company is somehow in such a market and is able to grow alongside it. Such a company is generally not in need of transformation; but most companies are in low-growth markets and a lot of factors need to come together to achieve double-digit earnings growth. You need to be strong both at productivity (produce more or the same with less) and also have the capability to generate growth beyond the market rates. Easier said than done and indeed a major objective of any transformation journey. How to achieve this performance and more, year in and year out, is the objective of this book.

Understanding Nuances of Cost

Transforming a company involves the proper interpretation of financial information and understanding cost subtleties. This may sound elementary but it is extremely frequently misapplied. I go as far as to say that decisions based solely on financial criteria (particularly cost criteria) will most likely fail.

In fact, I have frequently come across the style of management that is based solely on financials and I have observed it to be exceptionally destructive. This behavior leads to disabling companies, something which some business leaders understand they are doing, but most frequently they do not.

How does this behavior arise? It arises because management understands cost but does not pay attention to understanding what you get for it. Ultimately, any business decision comes to the question of how much for how much. How much cost for how much benefit. The cost is blatantly obvious and easy to see. Frequently the benefit is not so obvious or it may be a delayed benefit where you spend something today to receive a larger payoff tomorrow.

To win the cost-benefit battle you need to have a long-term plan and a vision of where you are headed. More importantly, the assumption that all cost is bad is erroneous; cost that will yield strong benefits, now or in the future, is welcome. In transforming a business you will need to increase costs in some areas while decreasing them in others.

For ongoing success a business must religiously practice the equation of benefit exceeding cost. This is a simple concept but it is not always easy to achieve. It requires a lot of know-how and understanding of immediate and future consequences. This is where a strong, long-term strategy is very helpful.

To illustrate the above points, I offer an example I have come across multiple times. This is an example of an executive who is conversant with the financial numbers but does not see exactly what they mean and the implications of each item of cost incurred. He is an executive in a position of authority who lacks the total skills for the job and does not have an effective plan of where to drive the enterprise. This executive understands the importance of producing double-digit operating profit growth and is under the gun from his boss to meet the objective. The problem he faces, however, is that he does not know what to do with his business to drive it to higher performance; in particular he does not know how to get his sales line to be superior or how to intelligently reduce his costs without hurting the business.

This is an executive caught in a situation where he does not see a path of growth and his company grows at GDP rates at best; he understands that with low sales growth he will never meet the operating profit required. He thus unwittingly places himself in the same position as the company in Case 4 in the table.

He needs to reduce costs to make the operating numbers work and he puts forth a number of plausible arguments. He goes through a sequence of cost measures (usually the broad-brush variety such as one in so many employees must be let go) and in this way reduces his costs to meet his yearly objective.

Please note that this broad-brush methodology for trimming cost is deeply flawed. There is no strategic direction in mind; it is indiscriminate, the good goes with the bad and it does not reduce the amount of work needed to produce the output.

In practice this approach will naturally lead first to the removal of projects and activities that are necessary to build the business in the future. The first to go are areas having to do with investment in growth for tomorrow, such as developing new products and entering new markets. In the short term, however, the financial numbers look good. But in reality, the business has entered a "care and maintenance mode" and starves itself of future prospects.

Please note that in contrast, the company in Case 3 of our table reduces the amount of work or has found methods of enabling the same number of people (and other assets) to do more. In doing so, it has obtained productivity without sacrificing future projects.

Cost reduction removes cost; true productivity removes cost as it simultaneously maintains or increases output, thus achieving more with less.

Going back to our cost-cutting story, as these wholesale cuts are made, particularly in future projects, the business stands less chance of producing an adequate sales growth in Year 2. As a result, sales will most likely drop faster in Year 2 while in view of inflation, a lot of the other costs go up (e.g., costs of running a sales force, research and development, administration, factory overheads). So with margin sinking and costs rising, the executive has created an untenable scenario with the potential of profits plummeting even more sharply in Year 2.

As this type of executive sees it, the cost-cutting approach is again the only solution available in Year 2. The second broad-brush wave of cuts follows, except now the cuts need to be deeper and wider to make the numbers balance.

It is remarkable to me how many times companies in need of urgent transformation have gone through this type of treatment; the purported remedy for solving the profitability problem makes the situation far worse.

So what should have been done differently? And how do you handle this sort of situation if you have to rebuild the company after such a negative cycle? In practice our executive did not see what else to do other than cut cost, and he has left behind a very weak company. The actions that need to be taken in order to clean up behind him are subtle. These actions have to do with utilizing existing resources to rebuild the company by transforming performance through methods and approaches that demand no supplemental investment.

Performance Causes Financial Results

In the above section, I suggested that managing solely from a financial perspective and trying to back-fit results is not a successful approach. There is no question to my mind that being guided blindly by financial considerations will lead to certain failure. If management is solely concentrating on these financial considerations then it has missed a major point: financial results (and we do want great financial results) are just results. The cause of sustainable results is not financial engineering or back-fitting strategies arising from projections; it is performance in the marketplace and strong performance across the operations of an organization. In other words the cause is performance and the effect is the financial results.

Companies that do not understand this profoundly, especially in hard times, cross the line and reverse cause and effect. The outcome is very poor performance and the business will either sink totally or will need to be rebuilt on a new philosophy and along broader strategic lines than just cost.

However, there is absolutely no company that can operate without strong financial controls and by financial controls I mean the measurements that show how the company stands minute by minute with total integrity.

There is also a strong difference between financial controls and management control. The latter is what allows the business to operate competitively and take the correct actions to success. The cost-cutting executive I cited above has strong financial controls and can measure and report everything; but he has next to no management control. He unerringly guides his business faster and faster into a negative spiral, something he really does not intend to do. He is not in "management control" and the business simply keeps running away from him.

This is why the whole analysis on cost needs to start with the quality of what is obtained by the cost, and against the background of a comprehensive plan that pays attention to what is needed to succeed in the marketplace and make operations more effective.

Same Cost Base Can Produce Different Results

The balanced use of financial projections is essential to running a business. So is a balanced approach to understanding both what lies behind cost and the benefits arising from cost. In other words it is important to know if the company is getting value for money for the costs it is incurring, and if not, how the situation can be rectified.

To illustrate this point further let's consider a company in a certain industry that has a payroll cost of, say, $100 million and an asset base of $500 million; now engage your sci-fi imagination and think of a parallel company in a parallel universe. Both companies are in the same industry and operate with the same conditions. They have the same payroll cost and employ the same number of personnel with the same asset base.

The real company is struggling but its parallel is doing exceedingly well. The parallel company has managed to solve one of the fundamental problems the cost-cutting executive did not think possible to solve: instead of sales shrinking by 1% a year as the real company is experiencing, the parallel company is growing at 6% a year under the same market and economic conditions. Growth is having a very strong impact on the parallel company's financial results; it is simply thriving. It is reinvesting into its future and is in a strong competitive position.

So we have the real and parallel companies in the same markets and with the same labor cost but the effectiveness of the parallel company is much higher. What are some of the differences between these two companies?

Given that the costs are the same and the number of people and executives employed by each company is exactly the same, then the differentiator here is items that do not show on the expense account, because there is no difference there. Now this is a major finding because the parallel company is somehow getting a lot more for no incremental cost.

Parallel Company: Doing Better at No Extra Cost

In this section I want to identify a few of the areas the parallel company handles in such a way to enhance its results without incurring extra cost. These areas, in my view, are generally applicable to every single company; we will identify them in this chapter and pursue how to achieve them here and in future chapters.

A) Quality of daily decisions

It is very likely that the parallel business is much more effective in its decision-making and much more effective in its allocation of resources. It knows how to identify opportunities, how to divert resources to the opportunities that are most promising and how to stay agile and nimble in servicing its customers. Quality of daily decisions is one of the great leverage points in transforming a company. As you might expect, obtaining a high quality of daily decisions in the totality of an organization is not something that happens by accident. Rather it requires a lot of work, training and systems. It also requires a philosophy of how to achieve this level of decision-making and a methodology to get there.

The leverage of getting high-quality decisions from an organization is simply enormous; it is a fundamental enabler in the transformation of a business. It is also one of those things that does not add cost to the company; to the contrary it brings in a lot of savings, which means it reduces costs. Good decisions help direct investment (and cost) to the areas that will meet objectives, while poor decisions misdirect resources to areas that will never pay. An organization that is smart about its decision-making practices enjoys huge free leverage.

B) Appropriate structure

Let me introduce here another leverage point that costs nothing and yet adds a lot of value. This is the structure of a business which is the way a business is organized and managed. I see a lot of companies having difficulty finding the right way to get organized. They seem to be in a state of constant reorganization, always looking for that higher effectiveness or deliberately creating confusion to obfuscate bad performance.

An organization structure is a delicate matter but finding the right structure offers a huge amount of leverage; the correct structure simply is a force multiplier. There are five core considerations:

1. Is the right leadership in the right place?

2. Does this leadership have the right depth of expertise and behaviors to make the organization successful?

3. Are the lines of responsibility clear with clear accountability and transparency?

4. Is the structure itself, including span of control and duties, something that makes sense for the corporation and its business model?

5. Is it easily workable or does it require "supermen" and "superwomen" to make it function?

If the answer to any of the above is NO, then you have found a huge opportunity to gain leverage by addressing it; to do so will require clear thinking and analysis to find the right answer, but it will be worth it.

C) The model of running the business

Different circumstances with regard to market, technology and operations require different ways to run effectively. The way a business is run, the way it is organized in different sections, how these sections interact with each other and how the business interacts with customers and suppliers is defined as the operating model of the company.

For example, a company engaged in manufacturing electronic devices needs a different operating model than a company engaged in the manufacture of say, industrial materials. The way each business goes to market is significantly different as is its business cycle with regard to product life, product investment and product development. The electronics company is probably selling directly to consumers and requires consumer marketing expertise; the materials company is probably selling to industrial users. The electronics life cycle is less than two years, while the materials one is measured in decades. The investment to launch a new material can be a very large one, probably 100 to 1000 times higher than a single electronics product. Product development in the one case (materials) can be ten years or more, in the other (electronics) less than two years.

Clearly, these companies are in extremely different situations and you might say it is obvious they have to run differently. However, in my experience very few companies pay detailed attention to their operating model; instead their operating model is something that evolved over time. By identifying the key areas of how it should operate effectively and by closing gaps and developing the appropriate processes and core capabilities, a business can gain a huge amount of leverage. If a business is not doing well, the operating model needs to be examined and adjusted as this additional leverage can be obtained at no extra cost.

D) Alignment in depth

If you run a company, now is the time to run a small piece of market research and establish whether you have alignment. Alignment is one of those items that gets results at low cost because, when a company is aligned, employees know what the objectives are, what they have to do and what their role is. In these ways, they can be very effective at working with each other and not work, unwittingly, against each other. The market research is very simple. Ask the people who work in each department to answer a few basic questions:

• What are the first five priorities for this department?

- What are the priorities, in order of importance, for the company?

- How do you fit in them?

The same questions can be asked of the team working directly for you, no matter what type of team you manage. The differing results obtained from this piece of research can be astounding and will reveal the level of alignment existing in your business.

The larger the business, the more difficult it is to obtain alignment; indeed the whole framework has to be dynamic and flexible enough to adapt to changing conditions. Still, despite the complexity of the task, it is essential to the health and growth of the company, and there is no excuse for not working to achieve it. Alignment does not add to cost; to the contrary it increases effectiveness and reduces cost.

E) Process

There often exists a love-hate relationship between people and the concept of process. Some people absolutely love process and cannot operate without it. Others find it constraining and put it in the same class as bureaucracy. The concept of somebody imposing a repeatable way of doing things is seen as undermining creativity, but in reality this is not true.

The larger the organization, the more need there is for process and standardization. Process coordinates and choreographs the "moves" at each stage and sets the requirements needed to move on to subsequent stages.

Process takes on a number of functions that are indispensable to the effective running of a business. In particular it:

- Defines common methodologies and common terminology

- Sets out what must be done at each stage

- Establishes the criteria which need to be achieved for a project to progress to the next stage

- Serves as the means whereby new employees are familiarized with what they have to do and

- Embodies a teaching impact on how to get something done

Processes vary from business to business and must take into account the stage of knowledge of the organization and the type of tasks that need to be accomplished. Typical examples of high-level processes that can give a huge boost relate to new product development, sales, marketing, sales and operations planning, manufacturing, acquisition and finances.

A great deal of improvement can be obtained by implementing the right processes. None of the business processes I quoted above are simple or can be implemented overnight. Depending on the size of the organization, bringing on stream any one of the above processes will require people getting together to define what needs to be done and an implementation phase (which may require new IT systems). It may take 18 months or more to design and implement the processes so they take hold, although in some situations, results can be obtained within three months. No matter the length of time involved, the activity generally provides continuous improvement, so that benefits begin to accrue before total implementation. An example of such an improvement would be the development of a common language that happens as you establish processes.

Clearly process is important. However, like every powerful technique, it can be overdone and begin to reach the point of diminishing returns and beyond. This is where judgment is required to revise and update; the more a process is embedded in the culture of the organization, the more it becomes practiced. The more it becomes practiced, the less it needs to be strictly imposed (as it is getting done!). Energy can then be directed to new arenas to progress further the stage of knowledge, which in turn leads to more effectiveness.

F) Culture

A lot is made of the culture of an organization and a lot is being attributed to culture. Quite often culture is used as a nefarious explanation of situations and events people do not understand. There is also quite frequently a resignation to the notion that culture somehow magically explains everything: "This organization cannot be successful because it has the wrong culture." Notwithstanding these perceptions, culture is a powerful free lever in improving the performance of an organization.

To my mind, culture is a simple construct. It is how people react to the situations they face everyday. An organization in trouble will generally have a suboptimal culture for success. An organization that has been through a few bosses or rounds of cuts will for sure have room for improvement in its daily culture.

In the context of transformation, culture is a strong tool that can be directed to aid the result. There will be no sustainable transformation of a business unless its culture has been made effective. It is important to set rigorous expectations of behavior and demonstrate them daily to arrive to your targeted culture. This is transformation activity to hone in on early; it is very possible to radically change the culture even of very large organizations and obtain leverage.

By the time we are in a full swing in the transformation process (and certainly the first changes are evident within a few months, and mount up thereafter), members of my organizations display certain characteristics: They know what they are doing, they are task orientated, they work effectively in teams and they address problems succinctly and will not use two hours where one will do. In addition, they look forward; they think of alternatives; they examine opportunities; they are agile, systematized and organized and they pay close attention to their decision-making process.

Interpersonally, they are demanding of each other but respectful and appreciative of the individual; they know when to take risks and they are proud to be part of a team that grasps opportunities.

Concluding Comments on Cost

Strong management, and indeed transformative management, pursues strategies to obtain high value for cost incurred and to obtain higher output than typical from the cost. Transformative management does not concentrate solely on the items that show directly on the cost statement; it concentrates on improving high leverage areas that enhance performance and will only show indirectly. Such areas include quality of decision-making, the structure of the business, the model of the business, alignment in depth, process and culture.

··· Chapter 1 Main Points ···

1. Starting with the market growth potential of the market you operate in, establish the kind of parameters that will enable competitive delivery of earnings growth. In companies operating in markets growing at GDP rates or less, hitting a double-digit earnings growth will require sales growth rates ahead of the market and superior management of cost.

2. Although strong financial controls are necessary, financial controls do not constitute management control. Financial results are just results! The cause of strong financial results is superior performance in the marketplace and strong performance in the internal operations of a company.

3. A wholesale cost-reduction approach will soon become disabling; management of cost has to take place in conjunction with a long-term strategic plan; in some areas cost may have to be increased and others reduced. In addition, successful cost reduction has to do with changing what work is done, and how it is done so it can be done with less man hours. Such cost reductions are desirable and are called productivity.

4. To transform a business you need to identify high-leverage management areas in a company and ensure that they are optimized. The effective organization and execution in these areas boosts growth and implicitly lowers costs. In a transformation journey you need to identify and act on these high-leverage areas early.

5. High-leverage areas include quality of daily decisions, appropriate structure, the correct business model, organizational alignment, the right processes and the right culture.

· · · ● · ● · · ·

CHAPTER 2 IN CONTEXT

Looking and Seeing

• • • • •

It was now Week 3 of my job at Environmental and Combustion Controls, and the magnitude of the required business transformation was hitting me between the eyes. Solutions are never found by closeting yourself in your office, in staff meetings or by continuing to do the same things. So I organized a tour of a number of factories. Besides coming up to speed, I figured that I might find some ideas to help the cause of the turnaround!

My vice president of operations walked me through the factory in Golden Valley, Minnesota. This was a gigantic electromechanical plant the likes of which I had never seen before – and probably will never see again!

In a very sophisticated operation extending over 1 million square feet, thousands of different types of devices were being built. The products from this factory controlled the heating and air-conditioning systems of more than half the homes and buildings in the United States and around the world. The factory was fully integrated and made its own sub-parts. In addition to more than 1,000 workers, the place was automated with robots.

A production line was being modified, and I stopped to talk to the guys who were rebuilding it. To further my understanding, I asked a series of questions about the work: Why are you doing this? How long will it take? How much will it cost?

The answer was that the changes were being made to facilitate what was essentially a minor improvement to a product. The project would take months and would cost more than $1 million. In my view, the time required was too long, the change was too expensive – and for what?

Later, I talked to the product manager in charge, and it's no surprise that he found himself between a rock and a hard place. The competition was turning up the pressure, with new products with electronic capabilities. We were trying to hold the market with an electromechanical product, which felt like a futile effort because electronic products can be upgraded much faster and at a fraction of the cost. So, our efforts to make marginal improvements to our existing product represented a double losing proposition for us: We would lose the market anyway and also spend $1 million. I couldn't help but *wonder if I was witnessing a microcosm of what was happening to the overall business.*

After Golden Valley, I headed to Chihuahua, Mexico, where our electronics products were manufactured. The manager who greeted me was ecstatic. He had reduced the cycle time required to make some basic thermostats from 7 days to 2 and was holding a celebration. He asked me to join the celebration and toast the team.

This was not the most modern electronics line, and our people did not have much to work with between the product design and the equipment they had. But while a 2-day cycle time may have sounded like a reason to celebrate, it was indicative of poor design and manufacturing methodologies that were not streamlined. Usually, these factors result in high cost and poor quality. So, instead of joining the toast, I gave a speech telling the workforce of Chihuahua that I would not drink to the achievement ... but when they could reduce the cycle time to 30 minutes, I would be happy to come back and celebrate with them. It came as no surprise that they thought I was crazy and just about said it in so many words. I took that as a positive omen!

Getting the cycle time reduced to 30 minutes lay many quarters ahead of us, and it was not just about what this factory could do. But in any case I did return to make the toast, three years later, when the cycle time had been reduced not to 30 minutes, but to 10 minutes. Champagne was served!

CHAPTER **2**

Mr. New Competes
with Mr. Longstanding

Chapter Overview

Effecting a transformation requires the ability to look and see. Most people look but do not see; in other words they do not fully perceive the implications of what they are looking at or the underlying issues and opportunities.

A person new to a company or industry has the advantage of the fresh eye; a person experienced within an industry will not transform a business unless he or she can also see with a fresh eye.

The chapter discusses three critical areas–quality of decision-making, structure and culture–to illustrate that by "looking" you can ascertain how the organization ranks. The objective is to ascertain if these high-leverage areas have room for improvement as these could be areas to begin the transformation path.

Mr. New Enters an Unfamiliar Environment

Let's say your name is Mr. New and you have accepted an assignment to lead a business named Original Corp. in a market you have never worked in before. You are not familiar with Original Corp.'s internal workings or the industry it is in. Your first day arrives and you walk into the office with a lot of anxious employees who are trying to find out what sort of guy you are and what you will really do to the business. Rumors will fly as to why an outsider has been asked to do this job.

Normally, when such a decision is taken, the company is in immediate need of some new ideas because it is in trouble. You may be walking into a situation where the clock is already ticking, but you are the guy who must reverse the trend and produce results.

I have seen people in this sort of situation behave in different ways. Some shut themselves in their offices where they meet with a few managers, consult with the HR specialists and get briefed by the CFO to find the way forward. But, as Mr. New, you have other ideas and do something different.

During the first few weeks you actually avoid such closed-door meetings. Instead, you walk around and shake hands and observe how people respond to open-ended questions. You also take the opportunity to talk about your management philosophy, especially with regard to people.

By coincidence, on the very same day you received your appointment as President of Original Corp., a business you are totally unfamiliar with, Mr. Longstanding has been promoted to run Identical Corp. Mr. Longstanding is thoroughly familiar with Identical Corp., its markets and its industry, and he has had a long career there. Original Corp. and Identical Corp. are strongly competitive companies in the same market with identical competencies and profitability.

Mr. Longstanding reads about your appointment in the Industry Daily publication. He announces to his staff that this is a great development for Identical Corp., as you have no clue about "our" industry. Mr. Longstanding reminds everyone that he, on the other hand, is highly experienced in the business. He declares that Original Corp. is toast, the prospects of Identical Corp. have never been so bright and it is time to really kick butt.

Is Mr. Longstanding correct? Is he destined to win the race against you, his novice competitor? No. He is overconfident but not necessarily correct. As in any race, the outcome depends on how both participants perform; Mr. Longstanding's early knowledge advantage may soon disappear. In fact, if you bring along the right qualities and can follow the approach recommended in this book, and if Mr. Longstanding does not act with urgency, you are the odds-on favorite!

However, Mr. Longstanding can also win, but he will not win because of his initial knowledge. To win, Mr. Longstanding will have to shed the burden of familiarity he carries, start thinking afresh and also adopt some of the strategies in this book. His knowledge advantage will allow him to adopt these strategies earlier, but remaining ahead will require constant vigilance on his part and a fresh eye.

As Mr. New, you know you have no time to waste. You accepted the challenge because you bring to the table qualities that give you the confidence and the capability to pull the win off.

The first quality you bring with you is that you consistently work from first principles. This means you are able to break down situations to their essentials and synthesize them. You are able to see a problem from many angles and are able to find connections representing cause and effect. Further, when you see something you do not understand, you routinely investigate to ascertain relevance.

The second quality says that although you are not an expert in the particular industry or company, you are thoroughly versed in most functions and aspects of running a company.

The third quality is very crucial; over time you have developed and tested a definite management philosophy and principles of managing. To paraphrase Winston Churchill, "in situations of ambiguity, without having worked your principles in advance, you will get lost." As Mr. New, you will not get lost and you know it; this gives you the confidence you need to push forward fast.

Fourth, you have an agile mind and are a critical listener. By critical I mean you are able to readily interpret information and find ways to translate the unknown to the known. You are able to readily discern when information you receive is not good.

Fifth, you know when you do not know. You do not get carried away with plausible arguments; you readily know when your direct knowledge is exhausted. In addition, your instinct about the people you rely upon for information is unerring.

Sixth, you are keenly aware of how to measure business risk and have the sixth sense that warns you when decisions and initiatives are likely to go wrong. When matters do not look quite right, you have the confidence to apply the brakes.

Seventh, you know how to tackle the unknown in a way that reduces risk and enhances upside. The journey starts with knowing what to look for; it is in this arena you will gather the relevant information with a fresh eye and use it to formulate solid plans to push Original Corp. ahead of Mr. Long-standing's Identical Corp.

In fact, it does not matter if you are Mr. New or Mr. Longstanding; ultimately you need similar (if not the same) approaches to transform your company.

Mr. New is forced to start from a point further back. He needs to work in a highly systematic fashion and must cover ground fast. He has a much narrower margin for error and has to be an all-round business athlete with strong legs.

This book is written from the position of you as Mr. New because you face the longer road and need the more sophisticated approach. If Mr. Long-standing adopts the same approach he will remain ahead. On the other hand Mr. Longstanding has one clear disadvantage: he does not have the fresh eye, and he needs to develop the habit of looking at familiar situations from novel angles, a skill that does not come easy.

With the above in mind, I set out some considerations of what you have to look out for when entering into a position.

Knowing What to Look For

Let me start this section by stating that the vast majority of people look but they do not see. Their eye is not trained to see and they are not tuned into hearing what is being said and its implications. I believe that to be able to see and hear you need to know what you are trying to see and hear in the first place. Also note that I use the words Look and See very broadly in this chapter, and I refer to investigating and perceiving implications.

For starters, in your "looks" you are trying to ascertain how the company functions; you are trying to hone in on obvious gaps in the core capabilities and identify the gaps in the functioning of the company. In particular, you are developing a list of the kind of levers you can identify and employ to improve the company.

Let me review and give practical examples of how immediate, high-leverage action can be followed from these observations, along with paths for improvement, by discussing a few such target areas.

A) Is quality of decisions a potential lever?

The quality of the decisions of an organization is a major determinant of its success and, clearly, is a huge area of leverage. Decision flow and decision quality are critical areas that can be assessed quickly with a few basic observations. Of particular interest is the quality of decisions made by the senior executive team, as well as those made the immediate level down.

It is imperative to talk to managers in the organization at all levels to observe and hear what they have to say and how they say it: are managers clear in their explanations of what they are doing and why? Do they have a clear methodology of handling daily issues (and strategic issues) that arise in the business? If presented with the same situation on two different days do they arrive at the same conclusion? Are they clear on the implications of the decision to be made and do they understand the risk profile? Do they have a clear set of priorities? Do they recognize potentially complex situations with unforeseen consequences?

Impressions form quickly and sound conclusions can build within a couple of months. If decision-making is really weak, you will find a lot of general inconsistency about how to handle situations. A lot of finger pointing or answers which are at cross-purposes indicate lack of alignment or simply people who are lost and do not know which way to turn. If you see and hear this sort of behavior you have a lot of work to do to overhaul what the organization is doing and increase effectiveness. Fundamentally, however, you should be very pleased; you have found a major lever you can pull for improvement…if you know how to pull it.

Another big lever is the way the executive team makes decisions and how decisions flow within the team. Is there competence in place to expeditiously make the correct calls and formulate the decisions in the right context? One very telling sign I look for is the quality of briefing presentations I receive from line and staff working for me. If these are clear and thought through (which in a company not doing well this is never the case) then we are in a good place; if they are not we are in an even better place as it is a major opportunity for improvements.

Similarly, observe to see if the decision flow makes sense. Examples of decision flows that do not make sense include the line manager in charge having to get final approvals from a person who could not possibly add value or line managers who have the responsibility but not the empowerment. Two more examples are managers who have the responsibility, but do not have the intrinsic knowledge or experience to make the right calls, similarly, line managers short circuiting or ignoring key contributors to the decisions such as functions.

All these items represent major opportunities for improvements. These observations are very powerful and they represent solid gold. And the remedies can be implemented quickly.

One final pointer: if you can get people in an organization to talk openly and ask them directly what they think about how decisions are made, you will receive a lot of candid input. At some point, if you hear the same thing a few times over from different directions, it may be something of high leverage that needs to be addressed.

B) Is structure a potential candidate for improvement?

To the mind of many, structure is something that takes a lot of time to sort out and represents a leap into the great unknown. My own philosophy on structure does not have the pretence of super sophistication but is instead one of simplicity and workability. I find that simple and mundanely functional structures stay in place for many years because they are reliable and work well.

One of the most unworkable structures I have come across is that of the global business leader of a stream of business (a stream of business is made up of similar products; for example, selling low-end cell phones to consumers worldwide could be considered a stream of business and treated as one entity, separate from selling high end cell phones). It is not an infrequent structure and yet most of the time it is very hard to make a successful go of it. Let me give you an example that illustrates how hard it is to make it work.

In starting a new position I received a long presentation from my global manager about the state of the business globally, roughly half of which was in the United States and much of the remainder in Europe. The presentation consisted of some 35 slides and at about slide 31 the presentation started tackling the issues in Europe. I asked the manager how long he had lived in Europe. He said he had not but he had traveled there a few times. I immediately decided that it would be prudent to travel to Europe and visit the team over there. I was concerned about how this structure was working because I know that being effective on another continent, particularly Europe, is not for people who have not lived there.

Furthermore, if the decisions were made by somebody not knowledgeable of the marketplace then surely we would soon become disconnected from it. Disconnection from the marketplace leads to decision-making based on financial and internal considerations alone, which does not lead to growth and prosperity.

My visit with the European team was very timely. They were very frustrated and knew the business was steadily heading in the wrong direction but could not do much about it. They had no real authority and had to refer decisions to somebody who was a long way away and did not understand the real issues or the implications.

So going back to simplicity, a structure that allows for sound decisions (such as connection to the marketplace), will win every time. In this situation, the guys in Europe knew their markets and their products and needed much more local authority to operate. Although there was an element of global co-ordination necessary on a few issues, such as new product development, the management in Europe had the knowledge and sophistication to paddle its own canoe and needed the formal authority to do so. Giving it that authority released a lot of energy and achieved superb results.

Ultimately, the structure should not be an impediment to the company and should enable it to function freely as opposed to constrain it. Structure is not the lines on a piece of paper. It is about the competence and attitude of the people whose names are on the paper. It is about clear lines of authority, whether with sole responsibility or in a matrix. It is about manageable spans of control and doable tasks. It is about staying connected to the marketplace and also enabling efficient operation. In the example I gave above, my United States based global manager (an excellent manager in his field of competence) had zero chance of success. He lacked the basic knowledge and he would have to live on a plane year-round to get the job done. This was simply not workable.

C) What type of culture?

The right culture will enable the right results. Aiming to establish a certain type of culture is part of leadership and transformation. Now, leadership is a personal thing and the culture you may want to establish is again a personal choice. But there must be choice as otherwise a key lever remains unused. The following are some observations on types of culture I have come across to facilitate finding out your starting point.

Open communication culture:

Does the organization tend to tolerate diverse opinions (contrary opinions) from subordinates or are people of such opinions simply no longer with the organization? Personally, I believe open communication is very desirable and it is one of the areas I probe to ascertain if it exists. If it does not exist, I find people speak carefully, or they talk in "apple pie" terminology, or they just try to double guess what the boss thinks and repeat that.

Inwardly focused culture:

A number of organizations are terrifically in love with their own processes; with these companies, there is an implicit belief that the function of the organization is to execute these processes. There is also a belief that if these processes are executed, then the job is done and success is assured. This type of attitude is very common, particularly in organizations that have had past success and now follow formulaic thinking. These organizations are not too aware of their current standing or how customers feel about them. An organization like this is destined to fail while it basks in the process it knows best.

Productivity focused culture:

Productivity is one of the great pillars of success. But, when productivity is the sole pillar, it becomes a very disabling activity. It results in types of behavior that cause the fear of investment in the business, the automatic removal of cost without assessing the value created by the cost, the fixation with meeting some financial metrics (e.g., year-on-year cost must be down, whether or not it makes economic sense), a lack of understanding of the customer and regarding the customer as a potential enemy. In addition, employees are viewed more as a line of cost without balancing it with what they can produce if empowered. This is a culture doomed to fail, although it may take a few years to see the decline if the start was on the back of a strong balance sheet and strong market positions.

Limited market outlook culture:

Organizations that are not sales and marketing driven simply have a very inflated view of their knowledge of the market and are sometimes not even knowledgeable about their channels or their customer's customer. The head of marketing in such a culture believes that knowing a few of his primary customers (and not the total market structure) is sufficient to do a good job. The business has its own view of what the market is and what it expects; this view does not correspond to reality and customers are rarely consulted. Asking about processes and events that engage and consult customers will show what is in place with respect to understanding the marketplace and how adequate it is. Equally, detailed questions of how and when "our" products and "competitive products" are used and sold will also show the level of detailed market understanding.

Engineering focused culture:

Organizations that are very engineering driven are also evident; this is the sort of place where engineers sit around the table and design the kind of products they feel the market needs. The result is that the products are only useable by engineers. Everybody complains about them except the guys who designed them—and those guys have no clue about the problem.

Splintered culture:

Organizations that are splintered are also very easy to detect. Frequently, such an organization operates in silos that are out of sync with functions and general management. Finger pointing is common and there are no comprehensive, common plans that transcend the whole organization and help bring its total know-how to problem-solving situations. In practice, the organization's response to an opportunity is to have different silos go out and try to achieve individual objectives but not total results. The outcome is decisions where the "tail wags the dog", as they are based on the considerations of a single function as opposed to optimizing the opportunity for the whole company. Further, in a situation of difficulty (or a real crisis) the main consideration is how to allocate the blame to the other side.

Reactive culture:

Reactive organizations are also somewhat easy to see. Instead of having a clear path defining activity over the next few months, they wait for the monthly results to define where they are. The absence of forward thinking is palpable. A response to the question, "How are things going?" would not be, "If we ship to this customer this quarter then we will be over the target," but rather, "We did great last month and so we should be OK this month!"

Control culture:

In a control culture people work in an environment where they are not given any room for initiative; this is a common failure in the structure of many organizations. Over time, people learn to execute orders and have stopped thinking. It is a sad situation and a lot of energy can be released if it is turned around. Unfortunately, it always takes longer than expected to train and empower people to think for themselves and take ownership when they have no experience with ownership or thinking.

Marketing-driven culture:

Occasionally, you run across marketing-driven organizations. Most of the discussions in these organizations revolve around customers and these are the discussions held not only between the sales and marketing people but also among the rest of the organization. These are organizations that generally have knowledge in depth about their customers and have had a long interaction with them. Having such a culture is a great asset.

··· **Chapter 2 Main Points** ···

1. To transform a company you need to have keen powers of observation and deduction and be a good listener. If you are new to the business, you have the advantage of a fresh eye. If you are already familiar with it, while knowledge is an advantage, you need to stand back and find the way to look at it afresh.

2. To transform a company, you need to be armed with the ability to work from first principles, have a definite management philosophy, know how to measure risk and be cognizant of when you do not know. These qualities are always helpful, but they become essential if you have no depth of experience in the company or industry.

3. As a matter of high priority, you must ascertain a company's quality of decision-making. Clarity of presentation and purpose, no finger pointing, expeditious decision-making and clear decision flows indicate high-quality decision-making. Companies in need of transformation do not exhibit these characteristics and thereby offer a great opportunity for improvement.

4. As a matter of high priority, you must quickly ascertain and fix an organizational structure that is too complex, does not have clear lines of responsibility and/or requires supermen and superwomen to run it. In addition, the company must assign to each position someone with the necessary depth of knowledge, attitude and competence to perform a superior job.

5. Observe how the organization behaves to notice what type of culture it embodies. Begin the work of converting to the culture you want to establish. (Detailed methods and suggestions on how to do this can be found in Chapters 4 and 10)

··· **•** ·····

CHAPTER 3 IN CONTEXT

A Huge Asset

· · · · •

It was October 2002. I was three months into my new position in Minneapolis, and some solid conclusions were crystallizing.

We had a superior brand name, strong distribution and a great legacy but we were falling behind the competition with each passing day. Huge reinvestment was required and, above all, we needed time to reposition ourselves in the marketplace. On the plus side, morale was getting better and employees were finally speaking to me and not the floor! But when would we ever see better results?

The ironic part of the situation was people started to think I came to my new position loaded with money from Corporate. They saw me authorizing hiring and new investments. The reality was there was no money from anywhere.

To date, I had managed to change the organizational structure and work on pulling the "free" levers mentioned in Chapter 1. Although very helpful, these actions were not sufficient to turn this ship around. Unless we could win in the marketplace, we were doomed! And we would not win with the products we had on hand to sell, even if we vastly increased the sophistication of our sales and marketing operations.

In November, I made a critical phone call to a business leader with many years of experience in electronic design and assembly technologies. We had worked together for more than 15 years at Pittway, a company that Honeywell purchased in 2000. Pittway had world-class electronics capabilities and this leader had a level of expertise that was beyond anything in my new business.

"I need you here to lead our electronics excellence program," I told the business leader. "I need you to help us reach the state of the art – and beyond. I need to speed up execution. The good news is we have a great CTO in place who understands what needs to be done, so the three of us will lead this effort."

The business leader came to Minneapolis and spent a week assessing the situation with our CTO. The two of them acknowledged that we were way behind in terms of skills, investment and sheer numbers of people, but they thought a turnaround was doable if we could commit to bringing on board another 50-60 engineering design people to get started. Also, we would need to teach old and new engineers the techniques for design for high-speed assembly. In addition, we would need full-scale pilot lines, which would cost a few million.

Where would the money come from? Think about the giant electromechanical factory I described at the beginning of Chapter 2. It might sound paradoxical, but this huge asset – along with the perennially inefficient investments, misaligned to the marketplace – was actually our biggest advantage, assuming we could turn it to our favor.

"You see this factory here?" I asked. "It is consuming $30 million of capital a year, and the products do not have a long-term future. You can have a good portion of it for starters."

"How about the additional engineering talent?" they asked.

"You go ahead and hire, and we will fund it by eliminating our biggest current 'asset': Inefficiency."

It was a hard fact to grasp, but we were tying a lot of money up in our inefficient operations such as the factory I cited above. Our sales and marketing and the way we were serving our customers were not running cleanly either. If we could improve on them, the sheer size of our global operations and the sum of our inefficiencies represented our biggest asset!

Over the next five years, we redeployed money so we could hire another 750 engineers. Besides building up talent in the U.S. and Western Europe, we also made a prescient decision to globalize our engineering by establishing design centers in Eastern Europe, India and China. This action seeded expertise for global expansion later. In addition, capital for modernizing and expanding our factories was plentiful. We found it by diverting money that would have been invested in (nearly) obsolete technologies.

The torrent and quality of new electronic products kept Honeywell at the forefront...and all because we figured out how to stop investing in the wrong areas and start investing in the right ones.

CHAPTER **3**

The Role of Management Philosophy

Chapter Overview

This chapter discusses management philosophy and the benefits you can derive from establishing such a philosophy early on in your transformation efforts.

A management philosophy as referred to here is a comprehensive, consistent and active set of principles that guides your actions and decision-making. This chapter explains how establishing such a philosophy contributes to and, in many cases, is essential for, effective transformation leadership. It then goes on to review the elements inherent in a solid philosophy and present a real-life example of my philosophy at work within an industrial company. In other words, this chapter exemplifies how such a management philosophy is established and demonstrates how it functions to guide the transformational journey.

The Importance of Establishing a Management Philosophy

In a transformation situation, you do not have the time to learn what to do; you need to know what to do in advance. In situations fraught with issues and challenges unfamiliar to you, a strong management philosophy acts like a beacon in the night, enabling you to continually find direction so you can move forward.

What are the components of an effective management philosophy? In some respects the answer to this question is "it depends." It depends on the nature of the enterprise you are running, it depends on who and what you are managing, and it depends on the level at which your work is taking place. As I have now spent three decades in a general management capacity of industrial companies, my personal philosophy has been honed to run such companies, but most of what I have developed for myself is applicable to other sectors of the economy that run for profit.

No matter the nature of your business, a solid management philosophy–one that you can rely on during your period of transformation and beyond–consists of vital, non-negotiable components. Therefore, your philosophy must be:

• Comprehensive, so it can cover a huge range of eventualities.

• Practical, as it will be called upon to guide action daily (and because practicality is an integral part of logical decision-making).

• Consistent and repeatable, because given the same situation twice— and decision-making in business is rarely black or white—your philosophy should always guide you to the same conclusion (unless circumstances have changed).

• Flexible, so it can adapt over time to new situations. Flexibility does not necessitate changing your fundamental management philosophy, but rather it requires you to continuously test assumptions to determine if the philosophy fits the environment. Through testing and evaluation, you learn if and when it is appropriate to add details and embellishments to your philosophy so your business can remain relevant as it evolves and moves forward.

In Chapter 1, I mentioned a list of "free" levers you can access and use to your advantage during a time of transformation. To that point, a clear philosophy is free and it offers a multitude of free levers. Not only does a precise management philosophy enable you to find direction and identify opportunities (particularly in ambiguous circumstances), it also enables you as the leader to maintain consistent behavior. As a result, the organization has no doubt about its policy expectations; people do not become disorientated by hearing conflicting messages or by sensing hesitation or changes in fundamental positions.

Another result of having a clear, consistent philosophy is that the methodologies of making choices and of picking direction are consistent, repetitive and teachable. This latter factor is of paramount importance because no organization can be transformed without learning new information and procedures, adopting new behaviors and changing its "DNA" into something more effective. Therefore, a management philosophy that is consistently enunciated and demonstrated through daily decisions and actions has a major impact on the organization; it is a major factor in a successful transformation.

Management Philosophy and Ability to See

If you are serious about wanting to transform your business, you need to possess the ability to look and see situations clearly. If you do not have an ability to see, you will have to develop it to achieve success.

What do I mean by seeing? It is the ability to observe situations (and listen to situations), assess them correctly and draw the right inferences.

I have stated that most people look, but they do not see. This statement is derived from years of personal observation as well as extensive discussions with managers on how they either saw, or more frequently failed to see, some very large opportunities or problems. The world is full of business people who become mired in daily routine, doing what they have to do by rote, without the need or ability to understand what is really happening around them.

When it comes to business, vision—or lack of it—can mean the difference between success and failure. On the positive side, the successful entrepreneur's vision allows him or her to spot and grab hold of an opportunity nobody else sees and make a go of it. On the negative side, major errors can be committed in instances when nobody "saw it coming."

In 2008, we experienced the latter in mammoth proportions with a near total collapse of our financial system. A few people predicted the breakdown and made large fortunes by taking contrarian positions, while the majority suffered greatly because they did not foresee the house of cards for what it was until it collapsed.

Vision plays an integral role in business and especially in business transformation. Having a clear overview of what is happening in your business at all times is vital to your success. Seeing what is going on daily and arriving at the overview and understanding implications is an innate skill. It is also a skill that can be acquired and continuously enhanced through a strong practice of habitual observation and the comparison of the findings against an ingrained management philosophy and well-thought-out plans.

Management Philosophy Development

If you do not already have a management philosophy in place, you need to develop one. Here's a scenario that illustrates what I mean.

Let's imagine your car has broken down. Here you are at the side of the road, kicking the bumper and calling urgently for a mechanic. He arrives two hours later, opens the hood, looks at a few things and tells you this and that has broken down, he needs to tow it in and it will take so much time and so many dollars to fix it.

What is the difference between him and you? Well, he knows where to look and what to look for. More important, he has in his head a plan and a model of what fits where, how it works and how it all fits in the total scheme of things.

Does this example relate to management? Yes, but it needs to be broadened and enhanced. The mechanic was testing matters against relevant training and experience. He did not design the car; somebody else designed the car and that somebody else knew how to develop the fundamental design from principles.

In management, you are sometimes in the position of the driver, sometimes in the position of the mechanic and sometimes in the position of the design developer. It is easy to envision the manager as the driver, and in many situations this is adequate. However, during a period of transformation, the manager needs at times to be able to assume the other two roles as well; besides running the business day to day, he or she has to fix and find new direction. The more extensive the transformation, the more the manager has to assume the position of the designer in order to correctly rebuild the company.

Unfortunately, there are no prescribed parameters to guide you in designing your management philosophy, as it evolves from a highly personal set of beliefs and operational principles. But, you will need to find your way with it if you want to manage in situations where you are not fulfilling the role of the mechanic but that of the person who works from fundamental ideas to get something new established. To do this, you need to inform and create your philosophy through reading, learning and doing. This is the only way to develop what I call a comprehensive management philosophy.

Transformation requires the ability to identify and drive towards that something new. I caution that unless you have a well-established philosophy, you should not go into a situation requiring transformation (particularly if you are unfamiliar with it), because you will very soon become lost. Conversely, your ability to assemble ideas and actions quickly from principles derived from a well-established and well-tested philosophy will allow you to thrive in known or unknown environments alike.

An Example of a Personal Philosophy

I will now review six basic philosophy tenets present in my own management philosophy and demonstrate how each one influences my daily business activities. As you read, it will become clear how these tenets serve as the guiding beacon, especially in unfamiliar and complex situations. I am not sharing this philosophy in any attempt to indoctrinate or proselytize (as you need to develop a philosophy that works for you), but rather as an example of a holistic approach that has produced consistent results in different situations over time.

Tenet 1: The roots of a successful business are in the marketplace

Without a marketplace you have no business. As part of my management philosophy, I have developed a list of marketplace-related expectations for myself and my colleagues. Here is just a portion of my list:

• I have an expectation that my sales and marketing people and most of the other departments in my company and myself understand who our customers are as well as what they want and need from us. I have an expectation that we know what will make a difference to our customers and how their business will be affected (improved) by our actions. I have an expectation that we systematically spend quality time with our customers to ascertain what they need—sometimes before they even realize it themselves!

- I have an expectation that we provide the best value and the best products, that we treat our customers fairly and that we develop long-term partnerships. I have an expectation that our development process will launch no new products without extensive input from our customers.

- I have an expectation that we hold an in-depth understanding of our channels to market and who does what within them. This is easy to say and harder to convey (in a way that can be understood) and sometimes even harder to untangle and work out. Consider you are a supplier of a part that goes to making a machine that is then sold in a specific application in the manufacture of semi-conductor chips. Alternatively you are a manufacturer of a system that is then sold through distributors, who in turn sell it to a contractor who ultimately installs it in the consumers' houses. These are long chains and yet the fortunes of your company depend on your ability to understand, market and sell effectively through these chains.

- I have an expectation that we are able to segment our markets and serve them with the properly trained sales people who are able to carry out the complete cycle of the sale. I have the expectation that we will be able to support, as economically appropriate, the sales effort with in-depth technical support. I have the expectation that we will know how to optimally direct the sales efforts and, in particular that we choose to service customers who are well situated and who exhibit strong futures so we can grow with them.

This list is not meant to be comprehensive or exhaustive, but illustrative. My entire list is a powerful set of expectations that offer a clear direction to what I believe the sales and marketing efforts of the company should be composed of. My expectations enable me to manage with confidence, for example:

- From day one I know where to go and look and find out what is working well and what needs immediate attention.

- As I look, I know what I am looking for and therefore I can see very clearly where others may see nothing.

- I know what I am observing and where I would like to drive the company in relation to my observations.

- I have a consistent basis for communicating what I want to see achieved. I can therefore set expectations and begin changing the culture so it moves in the right direction.

- My expectations provide the platform for improvements; I will implement these improvements as I become comfortable with how they rank in relation to the other opportunities I identify.

Some of the improvement opportunities identified in the first 30 to 60 days may take six months to a couple of years to come to fruition as they are sequenced, and the necessary preparation for them is put in place to enable them to happen. But, if the leverage is large, the time, energy and effort you put forth to effect them is worth it. To transform a business, you will need lots of levers of various sizes, but ultimately you will need all their benefits to kick in to facilitate your way forward to the maximum extent possible.

Now let me tackle a question I am sure is arising at this point: Can it really be that easy? Well, it depends. If you know what you are doing and you are able to look, see and execute quickly, the answer is yes! If you have not done it before or never worked in the area you are transforming, you may not have the prior knowledge to guide fast identification and execution; however, there are almost always ways to discover what you need to know and how to proceed.

Let me offer a practical example. Two of the most important and related, yet difficult to track, aspects of marketing involve understanding the reach your products have in the marketplace and knowing whether or not all potential customers have the opportunity to buy from you.

In the consumer-goods business for instance, there is always a great emphasis on obtaining strong presence in distribution (i.e., the outlets that the consumer goes and visits to buy goods), as without this you do not have full market coverage. If you do not achieve a high retail presence this is a suboptimal position to be in. In other words, you are leaving a major opportunity on the table because you are not reaching all prospects possible.

A few years ago, I was running a business in an industry where the structure of the channel to the end consumer was totally unfamiliar to me. The structure was similar to the example I mentioned previously in that we were selling to distributors, who in turn were selling to contractors, who in turn were selling (sometimes with the aid of architects or specifiers) to the consumer. Now, I did not know what our coverage was in this market and when I asked the sales and marketing people (all good people) they did not know the answer to the question either. A few did not even understand the question, and I believe almost all did not understand its implications.

I then started traveling extensively with our sales people and visiting customers trying to understand what was going on in this market. For more than 18 months, I did not gain any new appreciable knowledge of our market, no matter how many marketing experts I met and spoke with. However, I remained determined to uncover the information I needed; I realized there might be a huge opportunity for growth potential. As my research progressed, I learned there were no established monitoring agencies measuring this market and yet the market was far too large to be known by experience.

Finally, I found out that specialists had developed a quantitative methodology to solve similar problems and that this methodology could be adapted to address this particular problem, but not easily. After enlisting a year's worth of help from the very people who developed the measurement methodology, we had our answer, and it was astonishing. Our research told us that this mature market offered many opportunities we had been missing. We moved from thinking this market had limited growth prospects to learning we had barely scratched the surface of its marketing potential!

After implementing a strong program, we transformed ourselves into a company with lots of growth. To put it starkly, despite our sophistication and global presence, before this investigation we were aware of only a small subsegment of the key customers we could serve. However, now we were able to develop a detailed market-map; from this we pinpointed the parts of the market we were not reaching. In fact, we were amazed to discover we had not tapped into more than 60% of the profitable market within our reach. This was a momentous discovery that took a total of 30 months, but it was a seminal event in the history of the company. As a result, an old company was reborn, and redefined with a new lease on life; the company enjoyed a huge potential for growth and it became clear we could actually more than double our sales!

It is important to keep this in mind: without the philosophy in place, I would have never looked, never had been so insistent and never found!

Tenet 2: Strength in technology

It is difficult to overestimate the role of technology in achieving success and in establishing competitive advantage. Even if you are not a fan of technology, it is important to understand its power, its potential and the dangers it poses. For me, technology is not just another dimension of running a business; it is a tool I want available to my company and I want it available to a degree far greater than what is available to my competitors.

One of the key activities I undertake as I step into a management role is to assess where we stand in relation to technology. I want to know how we compare in this area to our competition and what we can do if we push the envelope. From these assessments, I like to plot a path (which, by nature, may take a number of years) to strengthen our technological position and, if at all possible, wrest leadership. I am such a believer in technology that this activity is second nature to me and I orientate my management systems and the way I run a business to achieve technological leadership. It is not something I consider negotiable, but rather an inexorable direction I follow.

Why is technology so important? There are few arenas in which you can discover (or rather invent) so much while also extracting so much value from your discovery. Just as you can strike oil or discover a mine, you can learn to systematically extract value, year in and year out from research labs, from systematic methods of product development and from a well-developed machine of new product introductions.

In addition, you can extract value by ensuring that the technology you employ, whether in your labs or in production or IT or other systems, is a strong enabler and a contributor to success.

Is there something that mitigates my love of technology? The answer is yes, but this something also ensures we obtain the full impact from technology. This something is economic viability. A technology will only be successful if and when it leads to products that are economically viable and that people want to buy. This generally means that the new technology will have to offer more options than currently exist and at an equal or (preferably) lower cost than available through other means.

In some cases, the enabler is technology and in others it is science. If you do not have the correct investment in technology (e.g., labs or instruments) you will not be able to develop the science needed to fuel future technology.

It also should be noted that the development and sale of technology products require alignment in many areas. This process starts with the ability to understand where the technology is headed and is combined with clear market requirements to arrive at the best product specifications possible. At this point, the engineering design team has to have the ability to design at the prescribed level and to work with the production team to ensure that the production technologies and methods are capable of producing the desired products. Finally, these products have to be manufactured consistently within these predetermined parameters.

Let me give you an example of how all these items coalesce. Upon starting a new position I had a presentation concerning our electronics product line. These products did not appear to me to be state of the art; they were clunky and unattractive with limited functionality. Besides this being an anathema to a guy like me, it indicated we were behind in our product development capabilities. We were not putting together what was possible and what competition was already able to produce.

The very next day, I visited one of our factories where the controller gave me a tour of the facility, including the relatively new electronic assembly machines we had on the books and of which the factory manager was very proud. As we walked the floor I only asked one question: What is the net book value of all these machines? I explained that I was asking because we would literally have to throw them out over the next 18 months and replace them with some real technology. The controller eyed me strangely and I could see he was ready to give the lecture of thrift and of not being foolish, but he was a disciplined person and held back.

The problem we were facing was fundamental and, if not addressed, would literally kill our company. Our engineers were using previous generations of technology to design products to be made on previous generations of machines that yielded products behind the curve. This problem was at the economic level; rather than representing "strength in technology" these machines represented the epitome of "weakness in technology." The remedy in this instance took a systematic effort to retrain the total company and reinvest over $100 million over three years.

But the economics were correct, the decision was on the money and we saw very large benefits with every new product we made using our new technologies. We implemented actions to realize even higher levels of technology with a determination and speed that left our competitors standing still, and we recouped our investment extremely quickly.

Now the question you are going to ask is did you really make this large investment by "leveraging existing resources"? Well, we did! To find out exactly how to do this yourself you will have to read the rest of the book and discover the framework of how you can methodically manage resources away from areas of low return, to activities of high potential and game-changing moves.

As a final comment on technology I would like to say, even if you do not personally believe in technology, and particularly if you do not understand what you can do with it, you need to be aware of what others will do to you with it. For this reason alone, you need to find the means to cover this base directly, or if you are not knowledgeable, surround yourself with knowledgeable people who can guide you so you do not get steamrolled by competition.

Tenet 3: Knowledgeable and empowered people

There is no leader who has ever declared (at least in public) that people do not matter. It would be a self-defeating type of statement, as ultimately we all depend on people. However, whatever the public claims, behavior regarding employees varies and results vary as well.

A place of work is not a holiday camp but, on the other hand, it can be a place where people feel they can go each day to make a contribution and where efforts will be valued and rewarded; it can also be a place people appreciate rather than a place they regard with total foreboding and trepidation. In my philosophy, creating this positive atmosphere is important and beneficial.

I need to acknowledge upfront that not every single individual is destined to be a good employee or enjoy (or at least not hate) going to work no matter how conducive the work environment. For that segment of the population I have no formula for success, and the best I can do is to have selection processes that avoid this type of individual. For the rest, however, which in my view happens to be the vast majority, I have as part of my philosophy an approach that management professionals find very positive.

My main expectation of managerial personnel is that they behave in a manner that enables growth and contributes to correct decision-making. In Chapter 5, I explicitly single out the behaviors to achieve this, including openness, integrity and the orientation to address in a systematic way the issues at hand.

A great way to create effectiveness in an organization is to allow room for plurality, including opposing points of view. This does not mean that once a decision is made the opposing views are allowed to continue; at the point of decision, everybody must rally and make it happen. The open process enhances the quality of the action plan and obtains commitment. Discussion and debate cannot, of course, be allowed to go on forever but they do yield commitment.

I believe organizations in which people are not encouraged to think will not be successful. In fact, organizations that are not used to the freedom of thinking are generally unable to do so; even when given the freedom to think, early results can be poor with potential for major errors. Part of my transformation philosophy concerning people involves teaching an organization how to operate with more freedom, while maintaining controls to avoid major errors. The processes and techniques I particularly encourage for correct decision-making are aimed squarely at developing a meaningful empowerment. You will learn more about them in Chapter 5.

Developing an empowered organization means being tolerant of failure that comes from well-meaning effort. It also means being tolerant of situations where the bets placed are not threatening to the well-being of the whole organization if they go awry. On the other hand, vigilance is required until the organization learns what kinds of bets make sense. It is worth noting that an organization with strong processes has the built-in safeguards to prevent major errors. Empowerment introduced with the institution of robust processes yields the best results.

In my transformation methodology, the operating mechanism discussed in Chapter 4 serves as the main teaching forum; it also acts as the progress-monitoring forum and as the backstop for avoiding major errors as the process of empowerment gets rolled out.

In addition, I say a system of values is also required. Nothing will show more in situations of ambiguity and nothing will guide more than a system of values. Clearly this subject could make for a very long chapter. However, there are three basic Platforms I try to propagate in this respect, as they make my task very easy:

1. In everything there has to be a consistent concept of fairness.

2. Nobody who temporarily has the upper hand should be able to abuse Platform 1, including me.

3. All conditions of employment have to be economically viable in the long term.

Finally, let me alert you to a large opportunity: much of an organization's psyche and culture gets forged in times of difficulty. In particular, leadership's behavior in times of difficulty has a major impact on long-term effectiveness. This is discussed in detail in Chapter 10.

Tenet 4: Excellence in operations

In the long run, no company is successful without the capability of being strong, if not excellent, in operations. There may be some special circumstances where a company has weak operations but, because of a technology lead, or a breakthrough product, or a patent or strength in other areas such as sales and marketing, the company can do well without the operational excellence.

A company also may be situated in a market in which cost of operations essentially do not matter because of pricing power by the industry. A couple of examples of such markets in the last few years include the unchecked costs of healthcare and of education. In the former the customer (i.e., the patient) normally does not even know how much he or she is paying; in the latter, anxious parents are doing all they can to have their children educated, an investment they believe will pay off in the long run. This perception has created decades of pricing power for all educational institutions. In most other areas, however, cost matters.

Please bear in mind that "operations," in the sense I am using it here do not include only the supply chain but most of the activities of a repetitive nature (for example as customers are serviced in a call center).

Operations is a huge subject. Whatever industry you are in, however, achieving high performance in operations will help tremendously. Improving operations and increasing productivity can become a very strong source of funding for any transformational effort. In particular, finding ways to improve operations (in terms of both cost and cash tied up) is generally something that can be achieved early on, even before, say, developing a new product or establishing a presence profitably in a new market.

Where do you start and how does someone like me impart some meaningful information in a couple of pages? Well, let me share with you a couple of techniques I use. First, let me remind you there is nothing like observation. Again, you need to know what to look for. When you have ascertained that, begin by visiting your facilities, particularly the ones with notoriety for problems.

At the site, besides holding a town hall meeting with employees, I like to walk the facility (if it is a factory) to observe the way the raw materials get converted through the process. I imagine myself being a particular piece part which arrives and then gets processed along with a lot of other parts into a final product. What is the importance of understanding this journey? If there is gross inefficiency you will pick it up in this tour of a couple of hours. How? If the raw material is moving nicely and the assembly is happening in a continuous fashion without stoppages, then everything is working well. If not, you have some correcting to do.

The time between the arrival as raw material and leaving the facility as finished goods is called cycle time. The time that the material is sitting in warehouses or is sitting semi-finished (but not worked on) between stages is really dead time. The time it is worked on is called touch time.

In a well-run situation the touch time is a high percentage of the cycle time, i.e., the dead time is very small. You would be surprised that even in a great factory the touch time is less than 20%! It is not unusual for this ratio to be 1% or even 0.1%. That means that only one minute in one thousand is devoted to processing material into product. The smaller this number the larger is the opportunity for major improvements. In a low-ratio (small-number) situation, a lot of uneconomic activity is taking place (nonvalue added) such as moving material, storing it and retrieving it for further work.

Changing low touch-time situations (like the one described above) takes time and determined effort, but even that may not be enough. It would likely require some investment, and may also require new technology development, extensive employee involvement and training. This is a long journey but very much worth it as it offers continuous improvement and continuous productivity gains.

Further, excellence in operations often involves a very tight linkage between those people who design products, those who develop the processes of how to build products and those who actually build them daily. This linkage is often forgotten; usually, factory people are blamed for not producing quality when the reality could be that, because the initial design is not robust enough, quality cannot be achieved under any circumstances. Again these are issues of major consequence and if identified early, can be great enablers in a transformation. Such improvements offer a strong competitive advantage in the long term and serve as a strong funding mechanism. And money always proves useful!

Tenet 5: Strong management control through a consistent operating mechanism

An operating mechanism is normally very necessary in running a business effectively. If you have the ambition to transform the business into something new, the operating mechanism assumes an even greater importance and gains a centre-stage position. The operating mechanism is not only the means through which the business is routinely run, but it is also the forum through which the changes are channeled and the new initiatives are identified, implemented and monitored.

Because of the importance of the operating mechanism and its central role in the transformation journey, I devote a whole chapter to it. My operating mechanism is called Business Decision Week and, in Chapter 4, I explain how it works.

For now I will say that management control is the ability to know what is happening so you can stay ahead of the competitive forces. It goes beyond financial controls, which, of course, need to be excellent.

Besides the financial aspects of decision-making, management-control activity needs to integrate all the aspects of the business and all functions. In particular, management control can only be successful if the external environment and the markets are taken into account in the activity of staying one step ahead of competition.

Almost all of the ideas and approaches that are advocated in this book converge to one key point: you must enable a very effective and successful management control of the enterprise in order to guide it to higher performance through success in the marketplace.

Tenet 6: Superior strategy and risk balancing

It is helpful to regard transformation as the strategy and implementation of actions that reshape a company into a much more competitive entity. Like any strategy-development activity, transformation requires developing options, understanding their pros and cons and then selecting a few to concentrate on. Not everybody in an organization has the breadth of responsibility or resources at his or her command to affect a companywide strategy.

Still, most managers have in their possession a certain amount of resource, and, in some cases, very considerable resources. It is a good discipline to demand that the organization in each area develops broad alternatives and selects a few for implementation. This approach establishes next-best alternatives and challenges established ways of doing things.

In the context of the previous paragraph, it would be very common to hear the word strategy being bandied around in all sorts of circumstances. I do understand there is a strategy for just about everything from selling, to buying, to manufacturing, to legal, to HR, to technology, etc. But lest there is any confusion, when it all comes together it needs to have a positive impact in the marketplace and put you ahead of competition. A lot of strategies may need to come together to create success in the marketplace but they ultimately need to add up to resource allocation and initiative selection that deliver the aforementioned impact in the marketplace. This to me is the "superior strategy" or the overall strategy.

There is one other point I would like to make about the overall strategy: to every extent possible, it needs to be different from that of your competitors. If everybody does the same things, then clearly differentiation, one of the great-value creation methodologies, will not be there. Now it may not matter that some of the other strategies (e.g., that of manufacturing) is similar to that of competitors. But, the overall strategy (when everything is assembled) would benefit greatly by being different and exploiting unique positions in the marketplace.

Finally, risk is associated with just about every choice, including the choice of strategy. Risk is one of the ultimate limitations to any initiative. Understanding this is crucial and recognizing risky situations is paramount to your success. Without recognizing the risk upfront, there is not much you can do about it. There is a need to understand it simply in an everyday environment and to handle risky situations routinely. For this reason I dedicate a good part of Chapter 7 to a fuller, yet practical, appreciation of risk.

· · ·   Chapter 3 Main Points   · · ·

1. A management philosophy enables you to see things that others do not and guides in situations of ambiguity. It provides consistency and repeatability. It enables success in a situation where the business itself is unfamiliar to you.

2. The philosophy needs to remain practical and relevant and be part of the daily decision-making. The philosophy may need to be adapted to different situations, but a strong philosophy is effective in a wide array of companies with only minor modifications.

3. A management philosophy needs to be holistic and cover the total scope of the business. The chapter discussed an example of a management philosophy that covered the following points:

   • A successful company has its roots in the marketplace.

   • Strength in technology is essential.

   • Knowledgeable and empowered people are key.

   • Excellence in operations is required.

   • Strong management control through a consistent operating mechanism is necessary.

   • Superior strategy and risk balancing are essential.

· · · · · · · · ·

CHAPTER 4 IN CONTEXT

A Moment of Inspiration

• • • • •

I grew up in Cyprus, an island in the Eastern Mediterranean. I never left Cyprus until I was 17. I couldn't have imagined that over the coming decades, with jobs in London and the U.S. running businesses with operations in both continents, I would cross the Atlantic Ocean more than 700 times.

To say I'm familiar with the flight between Europe and the U.S. and how long it will take to land from any given point along the way is an understatement. When there's work to be done on the plane, I can usually figure out nearly to the minute how much time I have left before landing.

So, you can imagine my anxiety when I found myself returning to the U.S. from a meeting in Germany with a gigantic problem to solve and only 2½ hours left in flight!

The meeting in Germany was on improving customer service and inventory management. It was typical. The room was full of strong people with strong opinions, but they could not see their way forward. They could grasp problems and dig into the details, but they routinely lost sight of what they were trying to accomplish.

Because this group ran all their meetings in similar fashion, the result was a lot of internal meetings involving lots of talk and increasing amounts of confusion. In this environment, slogans, motherhood and apple pie held sway. Obfuscation was the rule. Missing was an orientation toward concrete action and a practical assessment of options. Where was the ability to make things happen?

These were good people with strong resumes. I certainly did not feel like I needed better people in these jobs. But there was no way they could carry out the changes to the business that I was trying to make – and on which our turnaround depended.

The turnaround was riding on big changes in our go-to-market approach, the management of our products and our strategy for making investments. How were these changes going to be managed? How could I communicate with these people and develop their initiative to carry out these tough plans?

This was not a job that could be done by one man – I needed the ability to delegate and have confidence things would get done. Perhaps most important, I needed knowledgeable management around the globe who spoke the same "language" and thought about things with the same critical view.

Fortunately, inspiration struck over the Atlantic Ocean, and the way forward became clear. By the time we landed, I had the fundamental concept hammered out and explained in a memo to my leadership.

The concept was called "Business Decision Week," an incredibly powerful operating mechanism that will be covered in this chapter. Not only did it drive decision-making in a cohesive way, but it served as a teaching and development tool. The result was tremendous growth among my leaders in their judgment and that intangible quality called "business acumen."

Our great people became systematically focused and formidable competitors. Within one year, enhanced business acumen spread across our global business as participants began to teach their teams, too. We built efficiency and productivity into every aspect of our business. Our people spoke a common vocabulary – concepts they learned in Business Decision Week became everyday practices. The results kept coming in faster and faster. Now, we had the management brains and muscle to take second place to nobody.

CHAPTER **4**

Business Decision Week

Chapter Overview

Business Decision Week is the operating mechanism and the forum in which most of the transformation activity is initiated and controlled. This chapter defines Business Decision Week and explains how to establish and run it. Here you will learn the importance of setting an agenda, forum management, promoting attendance and quick decision-making.

What Is an Operating Mechanism?

An operating mechanism can be formal or informal. Its function is to run your business and enable decisions to be made in an effective manner. The operating mechanism must serve the needs of your business and run it by determining decision-making, providing direction and assisting and progressing all tactical and strategic issues related to the business. In addition to allowing the organization to resolve issues swiftly and effectively, the operating mechanism enables a systematic review of proposals and allocation of resources.

In many companies, such an operating mechanism is formalized. This formalization can be complex and multilayered, but it can also be as simple as scheduling an executive committee to meet on a regular, predetermined basis in order to make decisions and implement initiatives.

In other organizations, the operating mechanism is totally informal and irregular. In these instances, managers and team members address issues in ad hoc meetings and in response to burning needs; there is no systematization, and the information flow is limited to the individuals concerned and, even then, there is only narrow exposure to the operation and related information.

It would seem to follow that the larger the business, the more need there would be for a systematized operating mechanism. And yet, many large organizations depend solely on ad hoc meetings for the flow of information between management and staff and among management at various levels. A solid, systematic approach to operations, information flow and decision-making is far superior to the suboptimal ad hoc approach that leaves so much to chance. During a period of transformation, an ad hoc approach ceases to be merely suboptimal and instead can be deemed totally insufficient.

Demand a Strong Operating Mechanism for Transformation Activities

Transforming a business represents massive change. Quite literally, it requires guiding and pushing a business in new directions, teaching personnel new skills and creating a new organizational DNA. This cannot be achieved in an ad hoc manner; it requires the setup of a mechanism that will operate permanently as it effects these changes month after month and year after year.

You conceivably could think of these transformational activities as being separate from the "normal" operating needs of the business. But, if you step back and think about it, such a consideration would not make sense. It would put the so-called normal operation in conflict with the transformational activities. So, in practice, the two must merge and run as unified activity. As time goes on, and the transformational activities take hold, they begin to function as your "new normal." Over time you will discover that the major activity in the operating mechanism has automatically become transformation driven.

I have titled the operating mechanism I use for transformation Business Decision Week (BDW). This is the dominant operating mechanism in the company. Most of the management processes revolve around it, or, more precisely, they happen during it. BDW is a single forum responsible for:

- Running the business

- Coordinating activities

- Educating players

- Supervising progress

- Introducing new ideas

- Launching new initiatives

- Controlling the progress of initiatives

- Changing the culture

In short, BDW is a very holistic operating mechanism—an operating mechanism on steroids!

Considerations in Setting-Up Business Decision Week

Clearly I consider BDW to be an essential element in establishing the operating mechanism necessary to achieve transformation. And I imagine you are already wondering how you will ever carve out the time necessary to plan and execute a BDW. It is a fair consideration and one I have had to address when conducting transformations in the businesses where I worked. But, since I have managed to do it more than once, and with schedules as full as yours, I know there are ways for you to allot the time necessary to schedule a BDW.

To begin, you must ask yourself how much time you, as the leader of the enterprise, want to spend in running the operating mechanism. As leader, you have many objectives to accomplish and many constituencies and agendas. In addition to addressing goals and responsibilities at your business headquarters, you want to stay in close touch with your markets, meet with customers to hear what they are saying, and attend marketing functions and other events. How much of that should you do? The answer is as much as possible, although some people question the time allocated to this activity. However, if the number-one tenet in your philosophy is that "the roots of the company are in the marketplace," then you absolutely need to go out there, find out what is going on, bring the learning and the conclusions to the company and redirect resources accordingly.

Ultimately, however, any executive has one item to dispense and one item to manage; he dispenses his know-how and he manages his time. Incidentally, the same applies to the next level down and the level after that. So, in any operating mechanism, you need to come up with a system that is effective but very economical on the time of the leadership and of the organization.

Long ago I came to the realization that I have but a limited number of weeks in the year (my own target number is 10) to actively run a company. I know I must effect everything I want to accomplish (including a transformation) within that prescribed window.

I almost can hear you saying, "Wow! You mean to say you transform a company in roughly 20% of the time you have available for a full business year?" Yes, this is exactly what I am suggesting. I have achieved highly successful transformations within this 10-week time frame more than once.

To learn how you can successfully adopt my 10-week approach, let's employ a bit of elementary arithmetic. We will begin by looking at how a senior business manager like you might allocate the typical 20 business days available in your typical four-week month.

For starters, you will want to subtract one and a half days per month to account for holidays and some vacation, so you actually have but only 18.5 days left per month to run your business.

Let's say you run a global business and you're obliged to regularly visit your key markets, not just in the United States, but in Europe and Asia as well. If you travel a modest 100,000 miles each year, the airtime alone consumes 200 hours (a plane does roughly 500 miles per hour). Of course, there are 24 hours in the day, but generally 200 hours of airtime will occupy more than 20 days, and if you add travel time to and from airports, etc., you can spend 30 days per year, or a full two and a half days per month in transit. That leaves 16 business days remaining in your month.

Being in front of customers, suppliers, and attending industry conferences will eat up another five days, leaving a remainder of 11 days.

How will you use those 11 remaining days? I have not talked about visiting plants. I have not talked about the obligations to a corporation and shareholders and the time requirements of these activities. I also have not talked about the need to allow time to tackle ad hoc burning issues or time to study and initiate pivotal initiatives you want to introduce. There are other activities to take into consideration as well, such as acquisition identification and integration. Tending to all of this activity easily requires at least six days of the 11 that remain from your original 20.

Do the math and you will discover the truth of how much time you realistically can devote to business management and transformation. If you want to do a decent job, to stay informed and to not lose touch with the marketplace and the internal workings of your business, you have five days each month (roughly 20% of your total monthly schedule) to both run and transform your business.

The Business Decision Week Format

I have described above both the demands and the constraints on management time. By now it should be clear that unless you devise a system that allows you to run a business in 20% of the time, you will compromise your priorities, and ultimately compromise the success of your transformation.

Typically, trying to squeeze out time for business transformation in an unplanned manner is a management strategy that almost never works. More specifically, managers tend to sacrifice and compromise time they would ordinarily devote to vital activities such as meeting with customers; working out the strategy of the enterprise; thinking, inventing and instituting value-added initiatives; investigating new possibilities; and looking into new opportunities.

You cannot transform a company without undertaking these types of initiatives, without the introduction of the new ideas and without the time to plan and implement them. And yet, these are the pivotal activities that will suffer if you do not get organized from the get-go.

Often, the reason you are considering instituting a transformation is because your company is experiencing multiple levels of failures (or missed opportunities) that need to be addressed. Or, perhaps you simply want to raise your level of performance in a tough environment. In either case, you need to find a way to use the 20% of the time in a very intensive and regular manner and prime the business for improvement with very frequent review and action cycles.

The BDW operating mechanism I use meets the two major criteria I have outlined above: it only requires a maximum of five days (20% of business-activity time) each month and it is extremely rigorous. Further it establishes the cadence necessary to effect continuous business transformation.

In my business, we repeat this weeklong cycle 10 times a year. We have discovered that with every cycle, the progress is palpable. One whole week is a long time to devote to any one business activity, and consequently, each one of these weeks is intensive and exhausting. But, the time spent is always satisfying and the progress is always enormous.

What happens in every single one of these 10 weeks is the backbone of transformation. This is the forum where it all comes together and the whole of the enterprise is pushed to progress in a new direction. How you handle these weeks will determine the speed and success of transformation. And, depending on the ideas you bring, it will determine if you can achieve a progression four times greater than that of a normal company (i.e., achieve in a quarter what others achieve in a year). This is the speed at which I like to execute a transformation.

Agenda and Standardization

So what happens during a BDW? What do you talk about for a whole week? What is the agenda?

The agenda is 75-85% flexible and varies for each BDW. At the start of the process (i.e., during an organization's first few BDW cycles), I might establish the agenda 100%, but, generally speaking, input helps. It is advisable to set an agenda for an upcoming BDW about two weeks in advance by asking the leadership team for topics and then selecting from among those offered.

There are some items on the agenda that are in place each time. For instance, we always conduct a review of financial items–such as monthly results plus a rolling forecast for the remainder of the quarter and the year–and we always conduct a review of working capital items and cash flow. But once you standardize your agendas, these items do not take much time to complete (normally two to three hours at most), even for a global business.

Standardization is a key element in your first few BDWs. In essence, you want to establish what information to look at, in what form it will be presented and how to make the information most meaningful. This activity establishes the common language of communication. Once people get used to reviewing data the same way, they can see trends and draw conclusions very quickly.

Within the context of BDW, you will begin to notice that a review process that used to last one hour (with people drawing poor conclusions) now takes only a few minutes and allows participants to arrive at sound conclusions and alignment. As a result of such standardization, the efficiency and effectiveness of the BDW sessions rise significantly. This, in turn, creates the capacity to achieve much more than ever before, and with every session, the level and speed of activity increase.

Please note that the financial topics I mentioned above are essential to running a business but will not achieve a transformation. What will achieve transformation are those activities designed to push the company to new levels of performance. After the first few BDW sessions, which should be aimed at establishing a common language and installing essential processes (if they are not already in place), your agenda must be devoted to what will achieve transformation. This means you want to use the agenda to do the following:

1. *Launch and monitor projects designed to enhance capabilities.*
   Examples of such projects might include activities to decrease cycle time in manufacturing or improve sales-force operations. Please note these are not one-off topics but rather long-term projects intended to radically change capabilities in those areas that must be progressed over time. To become established, they require much time on the agenda; once established, they fade away altogether.

2. *Initiate strategic projects that increase competitiveness.*
   This includes systematically following projects to upgrade employed technologies or to monitor channels to market. These are not easy topics to tackle, but they need to be addressed, structured and progressed in order to improve your position compared with competition. These tough strategic topics are exactly the ones that, over time, will help you gain the upper hand, train the participants and deliver new capabilities.

3. *Use the forum to discuss projects with a widely applicable learning content.*
   If one of the teams has a particular strength (such as effectiveness in assessing foreign markets or customer service), this is the time and

place for the team to explain what it does and discuss how to disseminate the information to others.

4. Install sophisticated processes and achieve coordination in depth.

Depending on your business and your chosen strategies, some processes are paramount, and you will need to regard those as top priority and give them the attention they deserve to ensure they work flawlessly. It is no surprise that, given my business philosophy, I devote time to developing and maintaining excellent processes in the areas of technology management, sales and marketing. Again, these are introduced and maintained with BDW involvement.

Please note that nothing is fixed; the process of transformation is one of continuous change. So, your agenda will have to remain fluid enough to coordinate and progress with the change.

I would like to make one final point regarding the agenda: if you just look at the agenda, it may resemble any other business agenda (other than it is extensive). So, what is so different about this agenda?

Well here is the difference: the BDW agenda imparts a regular cadence on a business and embodies the ability to sequentially steer a transformation journey forward step by step. The BDW agenda is dynamic and follows the methodology and strategy explained in the whole of this book. At any point in time, it can appear to be an ordinary agenda, but when viewed holistically over time, it defines a path of enhanced performance and profitability. The whole company pivots around the activities of this week and the ideas, decisions and directions that emanate from it. These set the organization scurrying out confidently into new endeavors. The agenda and cadence allow for fast response to both opportunities and problems.

Most companies set out an annual operating plan, and my business is no exception. But, we upgrade our plan 10 times a year and up the ante with each and every BDW!

Attendance and Tone

When managers ask who should attend the BDW sessions, I tell them, in principle, as many people as possible but it is mandatory for my direct leadership team.

Of course, depending on the nature of the agenda, confidentiality will automatically set limits to the number of people who can be in attendance in any one session. Beyond that, if you are reviewing, for example, the way plants are running or a new marketing initiative, there is no reason not to have a large number of managers listen in. It is a learning experience and knowledge-transmission opportunity. If a sales manager has an approach to an issue that he has addressed in Europe, why would you not use it, if applicable, in the United States or Asia?

Generally, only a few of those attending will speak. However, listening in to lively discussions on how issues are tackled and progressed is a learning opportunity not to be missed.

BDW sessions encapsulate many objectives; they concern themselves with tactics, strategy definition and implementation while also serving to keep key management informed and coordinated. In addition, there are different types of sessions you can conduct. For example, you can schedule sessions especially for:

- Establishing new culture by setting out business requirements and expectations and by illustrating ways to approach the business of management.

- Introducing new information.

- Transmitting knowledge and new ways of thinking from one part of the organization to the next.

- Encouraging and illustrating best practice.

- Building confidence, encouraging the desired behaviors and creating a trusting team.

Ultimately, when viewed together, the sessions help establish common language, set company-wide objectives, outline programs and realign culture. These are the types of sessions that work to raise the bar!

The tone in these sessions is also very relevant. These meetings are not occasions for people to show up only to be shot down so that the bosses can elevate themselves at the expense of their teams. Such behavior kills the spirit of the endeavor and moves the business backward. Instead, each session must serve as an occasion to exhibit professionalism as you solicit input from the experienced participants around the table. If a presentation is flawed (and it often can be), it is an opportunity to constructively illustrate how it might be improved and request that the team return to the next BDW with improvements.

As we move from issue to issue in each session (most topics require a focus of about 30 minutes, including a 15-minute prepared presentation), what unfolds is a panoramic exposure to the affairs of the company. An enormous amount of learning takes place as these issues are resolved and progressed. This learning establises actions that become part of our procedures and DNA; this is what transforms the company.

Rules and Expectations

As a rule, for all items assigned to the BDW agenda (and that happens to be over 85% of the issues we have to address), I do not accept offline meetings outside BDW. I will not, for instance, take a meeting outside the BDW to discuss a project requiring capital approvals. Similarly, I will not take a meeting regarding resources for a new project involving research and development. Why not? The core principle at work is very simple: by virtue of BDW, we have established a routine and a forum where all such items are addressed with the appropriate people in an open fashion. All the key people are present, can comment on the matter and leave informed.

The reason this is called Business Decision Week is that decisions are actually made on the spot in real-time, and the business keeps moving along. Having one-off meetings and decisions only defeats the objective of this open system and wastes a lot of time. In other words, scheduling isolated meetings outside the BDW framework indicates a violation of and a disregard for the BDW format itself.

Another BDW core principle is very simple: all matters presented will be resolved in the room and a decision will be made on the spot. We make a yes/no decision on more than 90% of the issues presented. For the remainder, we give specific instructions on what has to be done for the matter to be brought up again.

You will not believe the momentum you will generate within your business when your personnel realizes it is working for a no-nonsense, action-oriented management team that knows what it is looking for and is able to make progress in real-time!

To decide most issues on the spot, you need to be a decisive leader able to develop a decisive team. However, being decisive for decisiveness's sake, will not lead to success. What is required instead is decisiveness with a high probability of getting the calls right. If you want to dramatically speed up correct decision-making (which is the backbone of transformation) I would strongly urge you to read about Enhanced Decision-Making in Chapter 5. In that chapter I set out a lot of the foundations of correct decision-making at the real-time speed we achieve. As an added benefit, once you begin this BDW process, including decisive and immediate decision-making, your team will automatically begin to observe and acquire these skills as well.

Establishing yourself as a leader who is in the position of having to make these calls in real-time may not be for you. However, if you follow the decision-making techniques indicated in Chapter 5, you will find that decision-making becomes more feasible, even if your style and temperament do not ordinarily allow you to decide quickly.

By now you may have surmised that a large part of the content and structure of this book involves putting you in a position to make correct decisions quickly. The chapters you have read so far, coupled with the information yet to come, are designed to help sharpen your visibility so you will be able to identify what is relevant and confidently and speedily choose the correct options.

When all is said and done, correct, fast decision-making is not easy and is definitely exhausting. I recall the first time I ran a BDW in a company where I was Mr. New. As we had not yet standardized our processes or communications (data was all over the place), my first BDW turned into a grueling 60-hour week of meeting after meeting where decisions had to be made and direction given. By the end of it, I was totally drained and needed a few days to recover. The good news is that the decisions we made were spot-on and, with each subsequent BDW, the whole process, including the rapid decision-making piece, became progressively easier. By the fifth session, we completed our BDW in less than 45 hours; 18 months later, we completed a much broader agenda in less than 35 hours.

By addressing issues in a timely manner, our company enjoyed a phenomenal boost of energy–something we were desperately in need of at the time.

Subjects Outside the BDW Agenda

It is true that some subjects fit more readily within BDW than others and it is important to know the difference.

Items that fit most neatly into a BDW agenda are core processes and issues of a repetitive nature that will eventually be spread throughout the organization. BDW gets hold of key areas and gives them visibility; it standardizes communications and sets out many examples of how to approach activities. At some point any situation, once it has been encountered many times, it becomes routine and can be tackled very quickly. When that point is reached the agenda needs to be moved on and extended to the new topics. As we have already discussed, new issues selected for the agenda are a matter of transformation strategy.

Not all subjects fit into a profile that can be captured during BDW (although I do manage to capture 85-90% of total decision-making). You may have a unique problem to address that is major and difficult, but that will occur only once in the life of your business. For instance, you may be faced with deciding whether or not you should partner with a company located on another continent. A problem of this magnitude is most likely multidimensional and deserving of much in-depth analysis. On the other end of the spectrum, you may experience a crisis that demands immediate attention. For instance, in the recent recession a number of businesses saw violent changes in demand. If you are faced with this sort of radical, sudden change of circumstances, what do you do about it and how do you react to it?

My favorite way of handling both of the above situations (i.e., a one-off strategic opportunity with a lot of complexities or a burning platform) is to hold a 90-minute meeting every other day. At the end of each meeting, you generate a list of action points and determine what information analysis is needed. People leave the meeting, tasks in hand, and show up 48 hours later with the requested deliverable.

I find that after going through this three to six times (with time allotted for background thinking between meetings) we get as far as we are going to on the matter and have solid action points and conclusions. Some strategic situations may defy a complete solution at that point. However, at the very least we have a strong appreciation for the situation, an interim plan and an idea of what to look out for over time.

I call the above process "hot housing" an issue. After we have reached a resolution, I will add it to the BDW agenda, as there is still much learning and information we can harvest from the situation.

Limitations in Running the BDW Model

Every approach has its own limitations or boundaries, and BDW is no exception. Before closing this chapter, it is important to look at where the BDW is not applicable or appropriate.

People who have attended my BDW sessions have pointed out that this is a great system. However, some also claim they would not be able to implement the methodology because of two issues. One has to do with personal temperament and management style; the other has to do with knowledge base, or rather the lack of it.

In the area of temperament and style, many managers feel uncomfortable placing themselves in a real-time situation in which they have to address a variety of issues on the fly. They prefer to mull things over and then arrive at a well-considered conclusion.

I believe this limitation is worth addressing, as the benefits of real-time decision-making are so great, and can be partially overcome by practicing the techniques advocated in this book (including techniques set out in Chapter 5 through 8 that help expand visibility). These techniques make real-time decision-making much easier, speedier and more surefooted. Nevertheless, if an attribute is not in one's nature, and/or if that individual is resistant to challenging his or her style, this approach will not work. Having said that, it is important to note that I have seen many people use my techniques to greatly improve the speed of their decision-making; consequently, their comfort levels with regard to rapid decision-making improved as well.

The second issue is even more serious. This has to do with domain knowledge. If you do not have enough knowledge in a particular subject (technology for example), how are you going to direct a meeting that demands you engage in rapid decision-making? In this case, many managers would simply appoint someone else to run the meeting or a specific BDW session. Nevertheless, as the leader you have a responsibility to attend and introduce key ideas at the right time. Besides, if you want to transform a business, you had better attend all the sessions of BDW, whether you are chairing them or not. It is better if you can chair the sessions, but you require knowledge to do that. If you do not have this knowledge, you need to hand the meeting over to someone who does, but you must attend as well. I also maintain that the more sessions you have the capability to chair, the more effective you will become.

If you are not able (i.e., you do not have the necessary background) to chair many sessions, another consideration arises. If you cannot chair sessions and are unable to coordinate discussions and conclusions, you have to ask yourself whether you can orchestrate all the activities required in a transformation. Honesty always pays and saves a lot of time and money.

· · · Chapter 4 Main Points · · ·

1. Calendar-time constraints mean that, in most situations, you probably have only one week per month to both run and transform a company.

2. Systematization is essential; combine the operating and transformation mechanisms and make them the center-stage forum of the business. This process, known as Business Decision Week (BDW), should be conducted approximately 10 times a year.

3. The BDW forum is where key issues are systematically tackled, initiatives established and decisions made. It involves working through real, live case studies the company is currently facing.

4. Broad participation is preferable; although only some participants will speak, every attendee participates by virtue of listening and learning. This aids the establishment of a common approach, alignment and culture.

5. To ensure clarity and brevity, it is essential early on to standardize communication and establish reporting systems, such as monthly financial and operating reports in all functions. This frees the vast majority of the time for new activities, for real business opportunities and to progress transformation initiatives.

6. Use the agenda to establish your selected transformation initiatives and to progress and control them. The agenda has to remain dynamic by continually introducing new initiatives and bringing focus to new areas. As your organization masters issues, you will move your agenda on to new topics.

7. BDW is the main forum that implements the transformation program recommended in this book.

· · · ● ● ● · · ·

Thinking Straight

· · · · ●

It was December 2002, and time for our first Business Decision Week. We held a session to discuss productivity improvement projects in our factories. The teams talked about a lot of projects and explained how everything was going swimmingly well. Presentation after presentation reported great results for each project. At the end of the session, the North American leader of the whole effort summarized the situation and its total impact on the business.

The results were extremely impressive. I got very excited. I asked our controller to confirm that the results were real, and he said they were – in fact, the results had been verified by finance!

A few minutes later, a disturbing thought occurred to me. So, I asked: "If these results are real, then why are the costs of production going up? Why is our gross margin not improving?"

We went around the table, and there were no answers. People looked lost. How could the business report all these great productivity improvements that weren't adding up?

We then proceeded to discuss the financial results for each factory. Apparently, we were good at noticing the good results that happened in each month while ignoring the poor results. Again the whole analysis did not add up.

One month later, we found ourselves back at the table in our next Business Decision Week. The explanation of the financials became worse. Were we indulging in a massive exercise in self-delusion? It's hard to believe that management enjoyed hearing about improvements that weren't manifesting themselves in the numbers. What was the reality here, and what was the proper way forward?

I visited the factory floor and spent time with one of the productivity project leaders who had reported great results. She was a bright young engineer, and I found her hard at work, making all types of measurements. I then walked over and started talking to the operators. Did they know what she was doing, and were they all talking to each other? Their answer: "No, we do not work together. She is from the productivity department, but we run the line." This was a very illuminating comment indeed...our left and right hands were not working together.

Within six months, we brought in experts who were deeply experienced in Lean Manufacturing. They had the capabilities and tools to holistically involve operators in all productivity improvements. This initiative became the precursor of what is today the Honeywell Operating System, a well thought through and effective method of running factories that continuously brings huge benefits to the Company.

Even more important, we now have unambiguous, objective daily metrics for all our operations that show us exactly what is happening. We have a rigorous system that roots out phantom money and phantom results, and managers can no longer take solace in numbers and claims that are not real.

CHAPTER **5**

Enhanced Decision-Making

Chapter Overview

Few would dispute that correct decision-making is the key component to managing successfully. However, this chapter goes a step further to explain how it is possible to establish the conditions necessary to obtain enhanced decision-making throughout the organization.

Enhanced decision-making is the ability of an organization to decide very fast and get it right with a very high percentage of correct calls and an extremely high percentage on the big calls. This chapter sets out nine requirements for achieving enhanced decision-making. The chapter is not about decision theories or rational decision-making tools; it is about establishing the right organizational environment in order to obtain the correct decisions up and down your entire organization.

Requirement 1: Establish Openness

Decisions in an organization get made within the culture and expectations set by management, as well as within the structural constraints of the organization. For optimal results you need to provide managers and employees with a positive framework to express their views and arrive at the best decisions.

One of the fundamental prerequisites for correct decision-making is openness. What do I mean by openness and how do I suggest you ensure openness happens in your organization? Let's begin by looking at situations that do not encourage openness.

Imagine that an employee comes into a meeting holding an important view but is afraid to say anything because she suspects her position is not in line with that of her boss. She is afraid that if she expresses her contrary opinion, her boss will later call her into his office to complain that she voiced an opposing view.

The interesting thing about this example (which I believe happens daily) is that the employee does not know for sure her boss's position, but either her misperception or his behavior has really managed to gag her for good! I have seen many cases where managers appeared to encourage and accept arguments in meetings, only to call people in privately to tell them how displeased they were that such-and-such a position was taken. Clearly the person called in did not agree with the boss's position and therefore "should know better, wake up and get on the team." This posture does not make for good decision-making. It may win (or rather enforce) an argument in the short term, but it loses thousands of opportunities in the long run. It is no surprise that a lot of underperforming companies are run by management teams that, over time, have stifled their own organizations.

I know that many managers believe an inclusive style may delay decision-making. These managers fear that allowing people to propose contrary opinions and ideas will result in organizational paralysis, as is often apparent in many political institutions. These managers conclude that openness is an ineffective approach and, since there is one decision-maker, he or she should make the call, thus avoiding the potential for anarchy and chaos. But, it is possible to strike a balance between these two extremes— a balance that honors openness while also preserves the leader's decision-making integrity in such a way that, at the time of the decision, there is acceptance and ease of execution.

Openness also means that information flows freely and the facts are put on the table in their totality, without withholding and without actions to influence the outcome by any sort of manipulation. When framed correctly, openness is a great tool for increasing the effectiveness of any organization. Of course, it is important to establish guidelines for how you will expect and encourage openness. Conveying these guidelines when addressing a broad audience can be a strong way to deliver your message.

A final point on openness: it requires leaders who are mature and have the knowledge to contribute to decisions and the judgment to arrive at the correct decisions even in the areas where they are not experts. It also requires confident leadership that does not bet its ego on every single argument. Just as it is dangerous to regard winning an argument as a way to win control, it is equally dangerous to regard losing an argument as a personal affront to leadership; I heavily caution you against taking either stance.

The way you behave as a leader and the expectations you set regarding the open sharing of ideas and information will have a major impact on how these very same issues are played and replayed in your organization on a daily basis. You must ask yourself how much tolerance you have for contrarian views and if such views feel threatening to you; you must honestly notice if you regard a person who holds contrarian views as an enemy or a disloyal employee. You must decide if a contrarian viewpoint represents disloyalty to you personally and why.

In my role as a business leader, I do not require personal loyalty but I do require a high level of professionalism. I also expect that anyone who holds a particular viewpoint (contrary or not) is able to explain and perhaps document his or her reasoning, and argue the merits of his or her case succinctly. I do not measure employee loyalty by how much any one individual agrees with me, but rather by how hard he or she works to help generate good economic solutions that will further the company's goals and vision.

I understand, of course, that it is far easier for a leader who is knowledgeable and competent (as opposed to one who is constrained and insecure due to lack of knowledge or expertise) to allow for full openness. Certainly, no leader wants to be perceived as someone without the necessary experience for the position. But a manager in this position must be mature enough to embrace openness; otherwise bad decision-making will become endemic.

There is nothing wrong with a leader admitting ignorance and lack of knowledge (not to be confused with lack of intelligence). On the contrary, such an admission allows him or her to listen, gather data and work with the team systematically to arrive at the correct economic decisions. In fact, as I have usually moved into companies I know nothing about, my stock approach has always been one of humility combined with an uncompromising determination to arrive at the correct decisions. These attributes win big for the company and earn respect from colleagues. As you embrace and practice them, they can help you evolve personally and professionally.

When it comes to decision-making, there will be that moment when someone has to make a decision. If you are the boss you have to determine that point and make the call. However, how you allow opposing arguments to surface so you can arrive at that call fully informed has a major impact on how the organization will behave daily. The formula I use is simple: I allow a reasonable timeframe for key views to be aired and argued. If there is no obvious clear solution, I make the call. At that point all arguments are put to rest and everybody has to do his or her best to execute the decision, whether in agreement or not; contrarian views will not be held against anyone in the future. End of story!

Requirement 2: Playing the Field and Not the Gallery

In a game of football, as in other competitive sports, despite the large number of spectators, the professionals in the field know that the outcome will depend on what they do on the field and the direction they move the ball. The corporate game, however, is somewhat different and can really begin to miss the plot. Large parts of an organization may not have a clear goal of what to do or may confuse the direction of the goal line. Although objectives are formally stated, the real play manifests itself in the players' day-to-day behaviors and actions, and it is management who molds and reinforces these behaviors and actions.

Employees are not stupid and they observe what is happening. They observe who gets rewards and who gets promoted. In particular they note what those individuals did (or did not do) to receive the best rewards, how they behaved and how they performed.

Openness aside, I realize no one has ever progressed in an organization by maintaining a consistently contrarian stance toward his or her boss. On the other hand, one of the biggest modes of organizational failure, especially at relatively senior levels, is the issue of acting daily to please the boss to the exclusion of any rational or economic thinking about what is being done. This is what I call playing the gallery and not the field!

I have had employees who thought their main job was to second-guess what their superiors thought and cook solutions to fit their perception of what they thought their bosses wanted. In fact, I have worked with managers who began venturing guesses about what my position might be on particular issues when I had yet to formulate any views. After guessing, they would go on to shoehorn a twisted argument to fit what they perceived to be my position. This sort of behavior in an organization, multiplied many times daily, leads to terrible decision-making and a lot of wasted time. It leads people to make bad decisions and then spend long hours trying to cover up the genesis of these screw-ups.

The only way you will score goals is by playing the field. You must understand the issues at hand and analyze the economic opportunities and challenges. You must watch the ball and tend to the ball so you can systematically move that ball down the field. This requires players who are encouraged to look at problems with a view to finding robust solutions, unencumbered by perceptions of how their bosses might react.

It is very easy to detect an organization in the rut of playing the gallery. In that environment, people are nervous and always noncommittal; they sit on the fence, watching and waiting to see which way the boss will go so they can follow. They will be reserved and reluctant to present an analysis, even if they have one. They never talk of anything other than the perceived company dogma. They will hesitate when they see issues that must be addressed and will be very afraid to step out of line. While the behavior is easy to detect, the remedy does take a while to take hold.

The remedy starts with setting expectations of behavior, but this is the easy part. Reinforcement is more difficult as it demands consistently "walking the talk" and offering daily encouragement so team members can really dig deep and find effective solutions. Of course, it also takes an organization with the capability to learn to think on its feet.

Not everyone who is practiced in the art of agreeing with the boss can develop independent thinking skills, but most people can.

Requirement 3: Increase the Tempo and Manage in Real-Time

There was a time that news traveled very slowly, and people had to wait for the boat to arrive from another continent in order to learn what happened months earlier. Of course, we live in the world of instant information and visibility. People who never imagined the electronic devices of today do not know how to live without them and the instant access to information they provide. And yet, many businesses do not behave with the same kind of urgency. There are businesses that wait for the close of the month to know where they are and how they are doing.

There is huge value in speed and an even greater value in knowing where you stand at any one time. This does not mean you can or should course correct minute by minute, but it does advocate you develop methods for continuous appreciation of a situation and, particularly, early pickup of deviations. In this way, you dispel any illusions and do not indulge in any denial of where matters really stand.

One of the key ways to improve decision-making in your organization is for you to ensure the consistent flow and availability of relevant data at regular intervals. Relevant does not mean too much or too little, but the appropriate amount. Of course, in all of these situations, the presentation of meaningful data in a systematic and regular fashion enhances immensely the ability to come up with the correct conclusions. It goes without saying that solid judgment is required to act on any data received. In that way, relevant data and judgment in decision-making are inextricably woven together.

It may take a while for you to decide the structure of the data and format; quite often, the process first necessitates developing a common understanding of communication content and relevance, followed by data gathering, structuring and automation. Personally, I like to receive data on how my business is doing (in terms of sales, orders, inventory, collections and plant performance) on a daily basis. It may sound overkill, but because we have already standardized the data-flow processes, it takes very little time for the management team to receive and review the pertinent information.

If you do not have these processes in place, it may at first take you a long time to amend your computer systems so your organization can produce the data you desire, but the effort will yield terrific results. For instance, our ability to establish data on daily inventory results in our factories and warehouses completing all inventory transactions on a daily basis, thus avoiding piling or postponing transactions for the future.

Having access to such data daily means we are able to investigate and correct items that do not appear normal. More importantly, with the daily look, we quickly arrive at conclusions as to where we stand. Because my colleagues and I are looking at the same set of facts, we are able to think together. Even if we have a disagreement, a short discussion is all it takes to help us arrive at similar interpretations of the data. This constant shared awareness speeds up our decision-making and ups the tempo of our organization enormously. I have often said that one of the reasons we are successful is that we can turn on a dime.

In August 2007, we began to see a crack in the housing market, a market to which we were suppliers. The news out there was that there were issues with something called sub-prime mortgages and the financial markets were becoming nervous. We watched our trends daily and we could see that something really negative was developing. Of course we could have waited months for economists to tell us what happened, but we turned to our daily data, which was statistically significant as we sold broadly into the economy.

I caucused with my management team on the back of the daily trends and external information we had available. In the space of two hours, we came to the conclusion that, unless if we were losing market shares in droves, something seminal was afoot. All our market knowledge suggested we were winning market share, but just in case we were wrong, we adjourned for a couple of hours and phoned our major customers.

Our calls confirmed that our share was at least holding steady (or going up), but that the total market was in trouble. We used the next two hours to assess how our factories and open supplier orders were situated. Now, if you have tens of thousands of products and over 25 factories this is not easy to do, but we had spent a major effort (more than two years) to have all key data constantly updated and available. If the economy was indeed weakening, we would be in trouble with overproduction, too many commitments and too much capital tied up in inventory. We could not afford such an outcome and we had to forestall a potential major problem.

In the same day, we made radical decisions concerning our inventory targets, our expected sales targets and how to alter the way our factories were running. All our instructions to our operating people were simple, direct and in alignment with our agreed-upon procedures. Our actions were quick and effective; our data standardization and our pre-agreed communication terminology enabled us to issue instructions and slow down over 25 factories and a large number of suppliers. We applied the brakes immediately, avoided major problems and remained out of trouble. We continued monitoring using a procedure we had never implemented to this intensity before and kept adjusting.

The result? We were indeed able to turn on a dime and address the change in the markets. We not only acted in time, but way ahead of our competitors, some of whom did run into problems. This gave us major competitive advantage and kept us ahead in the game.

Upping the tempo means you have the data and the systems to know where you are and are able to change almost instantly. Real-time means you have upped the tempo to the point you have caught up with the present and have the means to know exactly where you are and how you are performing! Much like an army that trains for years to ready itself for those few combat days or hours, an organization, besides acting fast regularly, must be ready for when it really needs to execute!

Requirement 4: Develop the Art of Forward Thinking

There are many ideas that enhance the performance of a business but few are as effective as forward thinking. Forward thinking is a subtle concept that deserves explanation.

I define forward thinking as the systematic approach of thinking ahead and positioning a business to succeed. Now this may sound easy, but it is not. If you ask most business managers what is happening in their business, very frequently you get a historical recitation of what has already transpired. In some businesses that have been around for a long time, management may still be celebrating and extolling the virtues of a product or the work of its founder!

In one particular instance, the vice president in charge of marketing in a business spent 30 minutes extolling to me a product that had been designed and introduced 50 years before! The product had clearly been a behemoth, but by now it was obsolete and in dire need of replacement. He was not seeing the current reality and was eons away from forward thinking. He was adrift in the past, residing within the cocoon of his own internal perceptions. He had not spent enough time working out what he should be doing for tomorrow, let alone what should be the products of tomorrow.

So, how do you move from the past and into the present, and more importantly, from today to tomorrow in your daily thinking and activities? I believe the key to finding time for the future is to stay on top of what is happening today. I believe it starts with the real-time capabilities described in the previous section and in the operating methods advocated in the previous chapter on BDW.

When you have distilled the key areas of your operation and are able to instantly produce meaningful, daily data telling where you stand in any one of these key areas, you are indeed on top of your daily operations. This creates the breathing space the organization needs in order to think about the future and direct its activities toward it.

How many times have you heard a manager complain that his or her organization is unable to do such and such because all his or her time must be spent fighting fires. You certainly must avoid getting into firefighting and other distracting activities. Now, how do you achieve that? The best way out of a firefight is never to get in one in the first place! When you are forward thinking, you can sense heat and douse the danger long before any actual flames have had a chance to erupt.

It is a simple truth that most people do not manage their days well and so they run out of time to devote to thinking ahead and planning accordingly. The very act of thinking and planning make the brain ache! Not to sound harsh, but if you cannot escape from the past in order to develop the discipline of the future, management should not be your profession.

If you want to be in management, you need to find the thinking and analytical time to work out where you want to be three, six, nine, or twelve months down the road. As part of your forward-thinking strategies, it can be quite beneficial to habitually pose "what if" questions. Such questions can help you foresee events that could represent large opportunities or for large damage. In addition, you need to identify strategies and core capabilities you will need to maximize the opportunity and minimize or eliminate the damage.

Major success–other than by serendipity–only happens when someone spots an opportunity early on (normally before anyone else) and makes it happen with drive, discipline and determination. If you can instill this method of operation into your organization, your organization will do very well.

How do you encourage this sort of approach in an organization and how do you make sure it is systematically fostered and developed? It comes down to a series of "approaches" (financial and non-financial) and the questions you ask and the priorities you set.

To address the financial part of the equation, request that each of your operating units produce a rolling 12-month forecast of your business, along with monthly updates. However, the more effective approach is to use most of the BDW time to heavily influence the thinking of the organization, the way it looks at current projects and selects new ones. This affects the shape of the future. In practice this means biasing the agenda and allocating a disproportionate time on the agenda to identifying, qualifying, selecting and progressing future opportunities.

The more time an organization can give itself, in terms of analysis and action to tackle an impending problem or opportunity, the better off it will be. The key activity is to shape the future. The earlier you can begin this activity, the better. Whether you are anticipating opportunities or problems (and you should be scouting for both), your operating mechanism needs time to identify as many of these high-importance, future-shaping events as possible so as to enable their shaping.

Requirement 5: Acquire Subject Matter-Knowledge and Expertise

Whatever the effort to see forward, it will not be achieved unless you have specific subject matter expertise available; ensuring that these are present greatly enhances your visibility and decision-making ability. To illustrate, here is an example of a situation that can go very wrong without such expertise present.

Let's say you are looking at implementing a complex project, such as putting up a new plant in a foreign country you are not currently operating in, and you receive a presentation from some eminent consultants on how this whole thing will be put together. Milestones have been given, investments have been called for, key dates have been presented as a "fait accompli" and everything looks polished and certain. In an atmosphere of excitement, everybody is counting the big returns from the investment already.

But then something tells you that all may not be so rosy and you begin to doubt and question your enthusiasm for the project. You begin asking yourself a series of questions, such as:

- How good is the visibility of the people who have put this together?

- Have they done it before?

- Do they really have the right to be making these assertions or is this a case of a polished presentation and a lot of well-meaning self-delusion?

- To what extent do key people responsible for delivering crucial parts of the project have the necessary subject matter-knowledge in the technology, foreign country environment and markets involved?

- Does the overall leader have the depth to see and balance the risks involved? Does he or she know where to systematically look for and find potential problems ahead of time?

- Does he or she know which are the major "hinge" points?

In most complex situations subject matter-knowledge and expertise are essential and it is imperative to have team participants with strong expertise. Clearly, such an in-depth exhaustive question-asking/answering session should always take place before any decision-making takes place.

Although your knowledge base will never be complete and perfect, some of the biggest blunders happen because of "blind spots" in background information and know-how. You cannot have good visibility if you have the potential for blind spots in critical parts of an organization. Inadequate background, lack of understanding, doing things by rote as opposed to really knowing and appreciating limitations are telltale signs of blind spots that will turn out to be costly sooner or later.

Having subject matter-knowledgeable people on the team will overcome a lot of the issues outlined in the above example. Bringing knowledgeable people onboard before they are needed, and certainly way before accidents have a chance to happen, is by far the more secure approach.

Requirement 6: Establish Common Terminology and Processes

Now let's move to the next stage of enhancing visibility and decision-making. Again let me put it in a practical context.

Imagine you have decided to spend a day walking around your development labs and talking to various project leaders about what they and their teams are working on. You move from desk to desk and project leader to project leader; as you move, you receive various presentations and discussions on each project's nature and potential.

While you sense enthusiasm in some project teams, you notice that other teams seem to operate with an air of understatement or confusion. Team members in one project cannot even articulate what they were doing. You go home in the evening and scratch your head: are you better informed? The answer is yes. Are you informed in a way that is consequential and allows you to make better decisions? Not really. How much visibility into the future did you gain? The answer is none to very little.

Now roll forward 12 months and imagine making the same visit to the same project leads. Imagine, too, that this time the visits take a lot less time and you walked away with clarity and visibility. Why? Because this time, when you were speaking to people, you were able to make meaningful comments and give direction. Team members actually enjoyed the visit and, like you, felt they had really achieved something as they moved the ball down the field. What happened in the intervening 12 months?

What happened is that you established a common terminology and processes in the organization. In other words, you established a common language and a common way of looking at projects. You also established a funnel for the projects. A funnel such as this begins with many opportunities and has built-in phase gates. It is wide at the top, with many projects brewing, and becomes narrower as projects fail to meet criteria for passing the gates. The system dictates that work is to cease when criteria are not met and resources are to be reallocated to those projects that do meet the criteria.

From this new place, your conversation with the employees will be fast and the communication will be specific, for example:

"This is a Phase 2 project. To date we have spent X amount of money and we have contracted to complete this phase in another 90 days. What is holding us back from reaching Phase 3 status is the achievement of these specific technical objectives and the market-verification work. The financials are still not robust because we have not totally pinned down initial manufacturing cost; the volume projections are short in the early years by Y units and we are looking at some adjacent markets to make it up and feasibility of reaching these markets."

In line with the information provided above, you can offer specific, pertinent suggestions and you can bring more resources and expertise to bear in specific areas to help the teams. All in all, this is a visit that both informed and added value.

Beyond such visits, the executive team will sit down during BDW and look at the aggregation of these projects and their various stages and financials. BDW participants receive a panoramic view of when projects will see the light of day; you know what will deliver a relatively high impact and what will have much less impact. You have the data-driven means to prioritize resources and halt some projects to balance the risk.

In essence, you have future visibility of what the financial impact of these activities is likely to be in one, two or even more years down the road. Decisions ultimately depend on judgment, but now you have a basis on which your judgments can be made. You can set milestones and markers for followups and, as projects develop, you will be able to constantly and continuously enhance your visibility forward.

Without standardizing processes and terminology you will never get this level of visibility and will never have a clear basis of enhanced decision-making. With these pieces in place, your path is paved in diamonds.

Requirement 7: Organize for Gestation Time

I define gestation as the time required for a decision to sink in so you can examine it from every angle, and ultimately ensure it is correct. In Chapter 4, I advocated the BDW system in which all decisions are made in real-time. In this section I am advocating the need for gestation time. At first glance it might seem as though these two requirements are in conflict. But, if you get organized with the right approach, they are not.

In a large number of situations gestation is not required because of one or more of the following reasons:

- This is a common situation you have come across many times and know how the "play" goes.

- You know from previous analysis it is "directionally" correct and there is no appreciable downside, only upside.

- This is one of those issues where a definite philosophy comes into play and provides direction.

- It clearly fits as part of the overall plan being pursued.

However, gestation may be required when a decision falls outside the above boundaries, is consequential or entails a great deal of risk. Many organizations faced with this sort of decision either make one without being prepared or go through a long period of time where no decision is made. By that time, the opportunity may be compromised.

The key to making this sort of decision is to spot the situation coming down the pike, which you are able to do thanks to your forward-looking systems. As part of my own forward-looking orientation, I require major investments be aired at their infancy and again as cases are prepared and investigated. With all of our major projects, and with investments in particular, we systematically prepare a 90-day look ahead. In some instances, we may follow a risky situation as it progresses over the span of a year or more.

We use the intervening time afforded by this forward-looking process to assess these difficult situations and work on them before a decision must be made. This creates the necessary gestation time—something that is generally irreplaceable. An organization that has its act together in terms of processes and opportunity funnels can function in real-time and make decisions securely much faster than one that is just learning how to coordinate itself. The gestation time is built in to the operating process and is afforded by the forward looking orientation and systems. This makes for very smooth, timely decision-making where no opportunity is compromised.

Requirement 8: Do Not Get Caught "Cold" and Identify Downsides

For all the precautions above, especially in an unfamiliar environment, you are bound to be hit cold with something seemingly out of left field. This something usually appears to be very pressing! This is where you need to be on guard but you should expect that this situation will occur occasionally. It is the time to remind your subordinates that you do not like surprises and it is their job to surface this type of thing early and allow for gestation and a correct decision. But such reminders do not solve the immediate problem as a seemingly pressing decision is still required.

In these circumstances, I meet with my key people and consult with everyone around the table. I listen to the options and provoke a strong open discussion. However, usually this is not enough and is really the time to exercise imagination and invoke instinct, assess whether what is being said makes sense or if people are simply misreading the situation.

In my experience, there is always less urgency than people represent, and unless I reach a point of strong comfort to make a decision, I assign tasks to reach that point of comfort. As a general rule, it pays to table an issue where there is no comfort forthcoming.

I tend to regard situations where I am faced with issues cold as failures of my methodologies and operating mechanisms. However, they do arise, especially if you are new to a position and new to an industry.

Please note this is not the time to give in to collective decision-making, but rather the time to think from first principles. Because seven out of the eight people around the table think the same way it does not make the decision correct, especially if you are the eighth and final decision-maker. If my judgment disagrees strongly with the seven, and if there is no time to investigate further, I simply postpone or override, especially if there is significant downside potential in the decision.

To illustrate, I would like to give an example of a real situation where all these factors came together. After working in a new position for only a few months, my team called a meeting to discuss our buying forward a commodity. The team put together an excellent presentation showing the trends.

The price of the commodity had really shot up to unprecedented levels, but in the last few months it had retreated substantially. The team felt the price had hit bottom and that we stood to gain huge amounts if we locked forward the available curve. Our chief buyer explained that he was an expert and had been following the market for over 20 years. He quoted a number of Wall Street gurus and shared reports from major banks and major commodity specialists.

As the presentation went on and the enthusiasm around the table mounted, my instincts told me something was seriously wrong. Worse than that, I was totally "cold" and new to the situation, circumstances where big blunders can really happen. However, the buck still stopped with me. Immediately I resorted to "first principles analysis" as there was nothing else available, and the analysis kicked in to overdrive. Looking around the room I felt I was dealing with great people, but wondered if anybody is good enough to understand this market and read it ahead of time. I knew the answer was most probably no. And if such people existed, why would they be working for us and not trading daily to make a fortune on the commodity markets?

As the presentation finished, I asked the team two simple questions: "What would happen if we got it right and the price did go up again?" The financial guy very quickly whipped a large profit upside. I then asked, "What would happen if this was not really the floor?" The answer was a major loss.

Then I asked two more questions: "If the raw material goes up, doesn't it mean that both we and competitors will raise prices because of cost?" The answer was yes, so we were, to an extent, "naturally hedged" on the upside and we could continue our profitable operations. Finally, I asked, "If we were hedged at a price above market—if the price dropped from where our contract price would be—what would happen?" The answer was that competition would drop price, we would be stuck and we would register a huge loss. In other words the bet was not a symmetrical one. I explained to the team that I could not afford the downside and hence I would not authorize its request.

Some people became visibly agitated and started making comments that it would be better if they had somebody in charge who was experienced in the business. Well, leadership is exactly about these situations. I thanked them all and told them that time will tell, but that was the end of this particular discussion.

Within 60 days the price really did collapse and had we moved forward and signed the contract, we would have lost over $100 million in a few minutes of exuberance.

I did not know the prices would collapse. Contrary, to what my team now believes, I do not have a crystal ball nor do I have a great "gut." I just have a risk philosophy (especially when I am "cold") that says if I cannot afford the downside, at whatever low probability, I stay clear of the deal.

Requirement 9: Develop External Visibility

A number of the previously mentioned requirements deal with internal issues and visibility. Internal visibility is a necessary but by no means sufficient condition for success. What is needed to complement internal visibility is external visibility. External visibility is a whole subject unto itself. In most businesses, visibility in at least the following four areas is mandatory:

- Market trends

- Technological trends

- Competitive trends

- Governmental regulation

Each one of these requires full time organized effort.

Frequently, it is not possible for one person to cover all these bases and in practice you may need groups of people who know what they are looking for to provide this visibility to the organization. I require the leaders in my organization to have an encyclopedic knowledge of what is happening in their respective fields and to systematically pursue activities that maintain and enhance our external visibility. This information has to be fed through the operating mechanism so it can be inserted methodically into our decision-making process and become a solid part of every decision we make.

In many respects, customer visits and discussions with them of requirements and trends covers a lot of these areas. Not all customers are good at reading the future; some live totally in the past while others live in the too-far distant future (with views beyond an intelligent planning horizon). But there are customers and industry forums with a very good grasp of trends and that knowledge of what is required in a way that can be very practical and meaningful. You will want to spend as much time as possible with these people.

Let me give you an example of how this works. When I was in manufacturing of electronic products for (generally) industrial applications, it was always very useful to visit the consumer electronics shows. Why? Very simply, they had the volumes to establish new breakthrough technologies and in particular drive down the component costs. This made our next-generation products economically viable as we could use the same components and put them in our applications. So, by visiting these shows, we could see what the future of our products could be like from a technology point of view. Combining this knowledge with the comments of key customers gave us strong visibility!

In fields requiring more fundamental technology staying in touch with the leaders in the field is a very key activity for external visibility.

The Characteristics of a Good Decision

If you have these nine requirements in place does it mean you will be making enhanced decisions all the time? I believe you will increase your chances substantially but you will never be immune from bad decisions. It would be nice if, in addition to ensuring the above requirements, you could put any decision (particularly material decisions) through some sort of stress test to determine how well it will hold up.

Some people work very hard to find the optimum decision-making point. Others postpone decisions to gather a lot of information to be able to hit the bull's eye on whatever they do. I do not believe either of these is a good approach, particularly when deciding strategic issues. A much better approach in these circumstances is to make directionally correct decisions and to concentrate on the broad issues as opposed to start optimizing upfront.

Besides the issues I have listed in the above sections, my view is that inherent in a good decision are a number of preconditions.

1. A good decision does not depend on the external or economic conditions of the moment. Its foundations are not ephemeral and can withstand tests on either side of economic expectation. In other words, it is a decision with a built-in margin for error as it allows for a degree of things to go awry.

In practical terms this means I prefer to rely on strong trends, and undertake continuous market confirmation of these trends, rather than try to exploit a situation of special circumstances. It also means that I am looking at a plan that is not stretched in every direction to meet financial objectives, but one with something held in reserve (or preferably a lot in reserve) that can be brought into play to meet objectives.

2. A good decision is directionally correct and does not aim up-front to be correct at the detail level. In fact, trying to synthesize a good decision from the detail level loses focus quickly and leads to failure. It is best to base decisions at a higher level and then to ensure there are no impediments to detailed implementation.

3. A good decision, to the extent possible, is reversible. Between two decisions, especially when forging ahead into the unknown, I will choose the one that allows for flexibility and that can be reversed if things do not pan out. This may involve a higher cost but flexibility is generally worth it.

4. A good decision has a number of beneficial by-products and I always aim to capture those, although I never count them into my financial evaluation. What are such by-products that can offer a much better upside and make for a better decision? Let's say that you are looking at two alternative solutions for a new process. One is to develop it in-house and the other is to outsource it. The outsourced solution may offer fewer headaches up-front and less capital. The in-house solution, however, has the advantage of developing key expertise that will be useful down the road. In other words, it has development of key know how as a by-product benefit, making this latter decision–in a large set of circumstances–the superior choice.

5. A good decision balances the upside and downside risks; it avoids the situations where the downside can be catastrophic. These factors are best illustrated by the example I gave in Requirement 8 regarding the purchase of futures.

Initially, decision-making opportunities and the tradeoffs thereof can be very subtle, yet they can have significant impact on an outcome. Ultimately, a decision is an individual judgment, but this judgment can be aided and enhanced enormously by the approaches mentioned in this chapter.

The chapters that follow contain many more examples of how to practically use enhanced decision-making tools and how to take them to the next level to make solid decisions that will move your business ahead.

··· Chapter 5 Main Points ···

1. Creating an environment of openness in which views can be expressed without fear of consequences and facts can be presented unadulterated dramatically increases decision-making effectiveness.

2. It is important that the organization concentrates on the business at hand and its economics as opposed to wasting time double-guessing and creating solutions based on what they perceive the bosses want. Demanding an organization plays the field and not the gallery is the only way to score goals.

3. Develop the capability to produce relevant daily data, which concisely gives you the state of the business and your markets. Ensure your organization has everything to assess the present and can view historical trends instantly.

4. Train your organization to systematically think forward by spending considerable time routinely thinking how the next few quarters and years will evolve and by having definite plans and projects to execute.

5. Enhance forward visibility by ensuring subject matter-knowledge and expertise in key positions; identify blind spots and areas where there is lack of know-how.

6. Standardize terminology and processes, with opportunity funnels and explicit criteria for attainment. This affords visibility at the specific project level as well as in the aggregate; it also serves to enhance decision-making.

7. Identify difficult, out-of-the-ordinary situations early as part of the operating mechanism. Follow them systematically as they mature so there can be sufficient gestation time for a final decision to be made.

8. Use the operating mechanism to look ahead and avoid being caught cold on decisions. If this happens, assess downside, and if large, postpone the decision. If this is not possible work from first principles.

9. It is paramount to set up monitoring means for external trends. In most situations, this means covering market trends, technology trends, competitive trends and governmental regulation.

10. A good decision has broad economic foundations and exploits long-term trends. It is directionally correct. It has flexibility, is (if possible) reversible and is not all or nothing. It has a number of beneficial by-products. It balances upside and downside, and avoids catastrophic downside possibilities.

· · · · ● ● · · ·

A Strategic Insight Guides Us Through the Recession

· · · · ·

In retrospect, I could not have chosen a worse time to start a new job.

In March 2008, I took over as president and CEO of Honeywell Specialty Materials, a $5 billion business. The recession was beginning to bite and was becoming evident in our order rates.

One of the few things I knew about the chemical industry is that it can be viciously cyclical. I looked at historical figures, and during the minor recession of 2001-2002, the profitability of Honeywell Specialty Materials essentially collapsed!

The business had since been improved, but this recession looked like a monster. My boss was very laconic in our conversations on the matter, telling me, "I cannot afford to have this business implode again, and I need significantly better performance than last time!"

As an old hand, I know that during a recession, you need a strong ability to make trade-offs. These crucial decisions will not only get you through the recession, but will also determine how well you will perform after it is over or as the recovery begins. You can be a butcher and get through the recession with a disabled business. Or you can make your cuts with laser precision, and wind up on the other end of the cycle much stronger than your competitors.

As I thought about what trade-offs we would need to make, I realized I had a lot to learn about the business. It would be necessary to get fully immersed to find the "laser path" forward. Butchery was not for me!

As in any Honeywell company, we had great people and strong technologies already in place. This was a great place to start, but we needed something more than that to weather this recession. So, I launched into my routine: Establish Business Decision Week, talk to employees at all levels, travel incessantly to look at plants, and meet customers. Listen, observe and listen again, and ask searching – at times naïve and at times annoying – questions and keep learning.

Within about 40 days, a pivotal, strategic insight emerged from this routine: We were operating in many diverse global markets and technologies, and we were trying to serve them all with a broad-brush business model. Instead, we needed to operate the business with three different models:

1. *Fast-Cycle Application Product Development, which takes an expansive view of opportunities, focuses on the most profitable applications and brings them to market rapidly – usually within 12-24 months.*

2. *Large Molecule/Scale-Up, which seeks advantaged cost positions and long-term productivity, supported by strong intellectual property positions and the required capabilities to scale-up inventions from the laboratory to world-class production facilities. This process can take 5-8 years or more, but once the new products are in place, they can last a generation or more.*

3. *Technology Leadership, which emphasizes deploying the best scientific talent to identify and capitalize on process improvement opportunities and commercializing process technologies that improve customer economics.*

Defining and focusing on three models would allow us to save money and increase effectiveness. Another advantage of defining three models is that it enabled us to put in place the enhanced competencies specifically needed for each model. This would directly lead to a lot more profitable sales. In other words, we could create more value for a lot less cost.

Like just about all other companies in the chemical industry, our sales suffered a 24 percent decrease in 2009. However, unlike other companies in our industry, our operating margin rates improved at the same time. Normally, increasing margins with such volume decline is an impossible feat. We not only achieved that but, in addition, we invested very heavily throughout the recession to build key know-how in our three business models. As markets improved in 2010 and 2011 the result was unprecedented profitability expansion, very significantly above historical levels and at the top of peer comparisons.

CHAPTER 6

Seven Effective Strategies to Produce Results

Chapter Overview

This chapter introduces a series of powerful strategies to enhance business performance. In Chapter 1, I discussed the importance of using free transformation levers to enhance performance at no extra cost; this chapter offers an additional battery of levers in the form of seven effective strategies that can be applied to produce strong results.

Each one of these strategies is extremely powerful and can (depending on the stage of competition) confer differentiation and major competitive advantage on its own. To be fair, it will take time to fully implement all of them. However, as soon as you begin to implement any number of them you will realize benefit that only will increase as the implementation progresses.

Strategy 1: Find and Optimize the Business Model

Different industries work in different ways. Also, companies in the same industry frequently operate in different ways and use different business models. Some of these models are effective and others are not! I know that this may appear an obvious statement but its significance is frequently missed. Undertaking the three-step process indicated below will pay vast dividends as it will lead to a more effective model.

1. Ascertain, as far as possible, the model that really operates in your business.

2. Arrive at a judgment as to whether it makes sense.

3. Modify it to what will enable the business to become a more effective competitor.

In my experience, people very rarely tell you what the model of the business actually is (especially in a business in trouble), although a lot of people will express opinions as to what they think is happening. Reality and opinions often differ dramatically, and to establish what the model is requires detective work of the highest order. This involves keen observation, extensive listening and questioning, imagination, calling on past experiences, analytical skills and systematic pursuit.

When people hear the term business model, they often limit their thinking to the financial model. In particular they examine the ratios between fixed and variable costs, capital and labor intensity, and cost ratios with respect to items like raw materials, R&D, sales and marketing, transportation, etc.

Although these are important to know and the financial analysis is necessary, it will get you only part of the way. More beneficial and in many respects more practical is detailed understanding of the company's activities and of decision flow. This is something you may not know day one if you are Mr. New and take for granted if you are Mr. Longstanding. Therefore it is important to pursue the objective of establishing an informed view on a defined time scale; there is no substitute for first-hand observations and meetings with employees and customers. This means devoting considerable time travelling and talking to both.

Consummate professionals often desire to "get everything perfect" within their business model, but as perfection does not exist, it is wise to regard continuous fine-tuning as a good alternative way forward. It is important to perform a needs assessment and prioritize from there. I always advise managers to begin gathering information on high-leverage areas first and immediately address those that are most seriously out of alignment. From there, I advise they target the next opportunities on their list of priorities and so on, until most everything has been aligned. This approach raises the questions of where and how do you start the detective work and how do you prioritize?

Your decision about where you place your focus depends first on the way the business provides its products and services to customers and second on how these activities are supported by the decision flow up and down the organization. In particular, you need to:

- Understand the dynamics of how customers are acquired and how new business is earned, or conversely lost.

- Understand how the competition delivers these same products.

- Assess and understand the internal organization needed to develop and deliver profitable and differentiated products.

- Understand how decisions are made and how they flow at all levels in the organization to support the above activities.

Of all the above, please note that the differentiation aspect is fundamental and the model needs to be positioned to achieve that. In addition, this objective needs to be fully supported by the decision flows. Differentiation is one of the major cornerstones to profitability and is discussed in more detail under Strategy 7 in this chapter.

There is no point in not positioning your company optimally for success, and the business model is a key determinant to that positioning. If you go back to the simple table in Chapter 1, the ability to maintain a healthy sales line is the most important determinant to success. Without a top line on the profit and loss statement there is no bottom line! You cannot rely on the general growth of the economy to deliver an adequate top line alone. You must have a business model that enables you to identify and acquire new customers or introduce more products to existing customers; this activity is foundational for success.

Clearly, the subject of business models is extensive but here is a shortcut: a three-pronged approach that will help, especially if you are in trouble. Concentrate on whether any considerations in terms of the model:

1. Add or subtract to the probability of acquiring new customers or acquiring more revenue from existing customers

2. Add or subtract to the probability of supplying a differentiated product

3. Improve cost

Your decisions will reflect trade-offs between these three criteria. Outstanding solutions will satisfy all three criteria, meaning they will increase the probability of acquiring new customers and that you will be able to supply differentiated products while decreasing cost.

The above considerations may appear high level, but they do give guidance into detail as well. For instance, you can follow the chain of how you develop and produce products and put them to the test. The test will indicate which of the activities you are currently undertaking add significant value.

In addition, here is an illustrative example from my own experience. In one of my businesses, despite the high level of capital and spend, we always seemed to be struggling. As we sat down for a fundamental review, our team soon got immersed (or rather lost) in very thorough financial analysis and projections. I asked my team this question: "What would enable us to win new customers and do so at a fast rate?"

At first, the sales and marketing team became defensive. They asserted that we were covering all the market, we were well known in the marketplace, and therefore there was nothing else we could do in that regard. So, I posed a couple of additional questions: "Why are we not gaining new business and introducing new applications ahead of competition? Was it a matter of our development efforts not being good enough?"

Suddenly one guy piped up and said we were not specialized enough in our applications labs and did not have the necessary equipment, people or orientation in the market-place to gain new customers!

His insight was key; when someone points out something so obvious and correct, suddenly everybody else sees the light as well. After some further discussion we came to the conclusion that we were not really set up to win new business and that, in order to win new business, we needed to improve and change a number of areas. Specifically we needed to:

1. Boost our applications labs in terms of capability.

2. Improve our customer identification and service in new applications.

3. Orientate our sales and marketing activities to new customers and applications.

To implement the above, we needed to make a number of investments, as well as reorganize and reorient the way we dealt with customers. Within a year, our efforts to change our business model began to pay off; a business that historically had difficulty growing broke out of its traditional customer base, grew rapidly and delivered a much stronger financial result.

It is important to note that your business model needs to be purposely designed to enable the business to head in the right direction. Your model will determine not only how you will achieve your results in the future, but also what you will achieve. The business model should be established as a forward-looking tool so that it directs the business to exploit the opportunities coming down the pike.

If you have the luxury of knowing your competition's business model and how it operates, it is worth taking that knowledge into account and consciously establish where your model is superior and why it will win. In the absence of that detailed knowledge, there is no substitute for orientating your company to play offense through an aggressive business model so it gets to new opportunities first.

Strategy 2: Size Efforts and Resources to Future Opportunity

In many companies and situations, the past determines the resource-allocation philosophy and practice of today. These companies allocate resources to the sectors that have proven to be historically successful. In other companies, there is no definite philosophy and things just happen as they happen. In yet other companies, perceptions formed long ago (particularly from mishaps) determine allocation and "this is the way things happen to be around here" is a frequent approach!

The most illustrative example of the resource-allocation opportunity I can make is in the area of sales. When it comes to assigning targets for the upcoming year, most companies take what a sales territory achieved the year before and add a percentage for growth. Now this means that in a territory where you already have a major market share you are looking to acquire a lot more, while in an area where the share is low, the target remains low.

While at first glance this approach seems logical, the potential for sales on the other hand is exactly the opposite. Low share territory is the one that offers the largest opportunity and is the one you should target with the higher achievement and provide for commensurate resources to enable this to happen.

If you examine different companies you will see examples of missed opportunities reflected and repeated throughout many areas of business practices; it is not limited to sales allocation. For instance, it is not uncommon to find companies that devote the bulk of their R&D resources to segments that performed well in the last decade but hold little promise for the future, while starving more promising situations that may be poised over the horizon.

The analysis that needs to be applied to make these judgments sounds simple but, in practice, it is complex and requires standing back and thinking from first principles.

You must be mindful that the whole of the organization is set up to lead you away from this sort of thinking. Those in charge of areas that already receive sizable resources can be counted on to both justify the spending and put forth solid arguments, usually with good reasoning, for even more.

Yet, if you limit yourself to these voices, you will overlook many areas where the opportunity can be as large or larger than those areas already receiving support. In addition, unless you bring your attention to these overlooked areas, it is unlikely, due to inertia and lack of expertise and skills, that they will be brought up spontaneously through the organization's existing channels.

The leverage that you can gain by deploying resource on a future potential basis as opposed to what happened in the past can be mind blowing. I have been in situations where the effective utilization of the sales force was 50 to 60% and I have been in situations where the effective utilization of development resources was less than 50%. The former involved spending an inordinate amount of time visiting those customers where we could not possibly attract more business at the expense of customers where we had much better prospects for additional business. The latter involved efforts to improve passé products. Even if tinkering with these products had resulted in improvements, it would not possibly have made any difference as the markets had already moved on.

Such shifts in focus and related activities cannot be implemented overnight, but if you can facilitate implementation in reasonable time frames their impact is extremely positive. In both the examples cited above (one in sales and the other in R&D), the effect was to double the output obtained without spending even one dollar more!

Strategy 3: Reallocate to Win

Let's say that by now you have spent time examining various aspects of your business and you have begun using a number of different approaches to arrive at a view of what your ideal business model would look like. While the view you have developed is not by any means complete (and it will become more detailed over the next few weeks, months, quarters) it is time to set some actions in place, especially in those areas where you are already comfortable and where you already have some direction.

But what are you really looking for? Well, the answer is fairly simple! You are looking at assessing which capabilities need to be established or augmented and which need to be slimmed down or removed altogether. Now this is one activity that you do not want to postpone as with every modification you will realize improvement.

If you ask most managers what they need to improve their business functions and profitability, the answer will most likely be that they need more: more resources and more personnel.

While the above is the natural reaction of most managers, this is not the strategy to be followed if you want to transform your business. It is a reality that in a transformation situation you are usually short of additional money, but under all circumstances it is also a great discipline to assume you are short of money anyway. It is for these reasons that the general augmentation of resource is not the first item on the agenda.

In general a three-step process has to be followed that culminates, in the third step, with the areas where you are looking to strategically augment the capability of the business. The augmentation targets are the areas that will enable the capture of market opportunity and contribute to the establishment of game-changing moves. (The definition and explanation of "game-changing moves" is in Chapter 8, but for the time being it is enough to assume that they are material initiatives that will greatly improve the competitiveness of your business.)

However, the first step in the process is the full and effective use of current resources. Before you spend one cent, you should ask yourself

- How much more effectiveness can I obtain with existing assets?

- How much more can I achieve by applying some of the techniques already discussed in this book?

- How much more "capacity" can I deliver from existing assets (human and physical) by redirection alone?

- How much more effective can I become by exercising better organization and concentration behind the key objectives only?

- How much more can I achieve by raising the levels of competence and expertise?

The second step suggests you systematically identify areas that do not make economic sense; you then start slimming them down. Such identification may result in many different solutions, e.g., revamping a structure that is not conducive to good decision-making, eliminating overlaps and functional redundancies, revisiting or eliminating projects that are ill conceived or situations that do not have a high probability of success (particularly if the outcome, even if successful, is not material), cutting exorbitant costs, and addressing areas where costs can be removed.

You need to attack these areas with surety, gusto and a consistent message: uneconomic areas do not have a future in this enterprise. This is a good message to spread to the management teams. I find, once management team members get into the spirit of the effort, they begin brainstorming creative ideas in keeping with this message. When ideas bubble up, I still expect my managers to supply me with the economics associated with each one so I can make certain the areas in which we intend to disinvest are not strategic. This also reinforces the message that the decision-making is based on economics and not on "playing the gallery."

Now, the third step takes place as soon as you implement slimming activities (or concurrently), and it consists of investing the "proceeds" in the areas that you decide need support or expansion and/or in totally new areas that become part of the new strategy.

This sequence of events, that can essentially be repeated any time, is particularly useful when starting a transformation journey because it is an effective funding mechanism. Within a few quarters, good initiatives will become themselves providers of new sources of funding.

The three steps I have described in this section are a formal process of resource reallocation. In essence by effectively directing the same (or even lesser) amount of resources you are aiming to obtain a better result. I have aimed many of the suggestions in this chapter at internal productivity or enhanced effectiveness in the marketplace. The reallocation strategy supplements these approaches and systematically moves resources from less promising to more promising areas, thus continually enhancing prospects.

Strategy 4: Introduce Investment Basics for All

In some organizations, a few people with a strong finance bias have a firm hold on the investment keys and criteria. While at first glance this arrangement seems to make sense, in my experience, it is a recipe for suboptimal results and represents a great opportunity for improvement. To get the best results possible, you must make basic investment ideas known throughout the organization. In addition, before authorizing any expenditure, you must establish and adhere to strict requirements regarding the full examination of alternatives.

During times of financial stress, people have an aversion toward investment; the tendency is to save cash even when it does not make sense to do so. During more financially relaxed and seemingly secure times, people tend to spend when it is not justified.

Your ability to recognize situations that warrant expenditure—and the ability to teach the organization as a whole to do the same—can pay off in huge dividends; if executed correctly, such spending leads to superior financial performance and capital productivity. The first step in this process is to go to great lengths to ensure that the organization understands one simple concept: payback.

In my business, I stress to my management teams the importance of looking favorably upon all situations that will give us payback in under two years. I also make sure my people understand that we cannot delay, even for one second, well-reasoned opportunities that embody the possibility of a very fast payback, for instance, within six months' time.

You would be amazed at the results I get out of a campaign like this. In addition to helping people learn the trade-offs that occur between operating costs and capital, a large number of good projects come out of the woodwork. Why? Because people who previously did not fully understand an overly sophisticated approach to spending—one that typically involves complex accounting and finance terms—finally "get it". Instead of getting lost in the intricacies of the financial terms, they now concentrate on the economics of the project and are now part of the solution.

Except when I am dealing with personnel at senior levels, or when I'm in the final examination of major projects, I expressly discourage discounted cash flow analysis. I find that when it comes to calculations regarding net present value (NPV), people at the working level quickly become lost and consequently lose touch with a situation's economic benefits.

A simple understanding of money going out and money coming in (which is what payback analysis is) is all that is needed to empower people who have no formal training in finance. Such an understanding enables them to come up with the correct conclusions and encourages them to bring forward good projects that otherwise would never surface.

Before any investment is authorized, I make certain we have already examined a number of alternatives and that we have taken time—serious gestation time—to air the proposal in a multifunctional team setting. In addition, any time we consider a project above certain investment limits, I insist that a proposal must, in a short form, present alternatives and demonstrate why the recommended option is superior to any other alternative on the table.

When these two simple propositions—payback and the practice of generating alternatives—are spread throughout an organization, they have major impact on the amount of money we spend, as well as on the quality of projects and ideas we invest in. Generally speaking, the amount of capital required hitherto is significantly reduced as people readily discover more intelligent and less capital-intensive ways to achieve the same or better results. I have now observed (in a number of disparate businesses) that this systematic approach typically releases an amazing 20 to 30% of total capital that can then be made available for high-return projects.

Clearly, with the above scenarios (lower absolute investments and higher return projects) the returns go up and the capital expenditure becomes a strong contributor to the transformation journey. It sounds simple, simplistic and even too good to be true, but it really works! As usual, if you can train an organization to think simply, effectively and correctly in its entirety, you will win in spades.

Strategy 5: Develop a Detailed Market-Map[1]

There is no marketing or sales person I have come across who has not professed a strong knowledge of his or her marketplace. After all, part of the function, is the ability to project an image and convince. Reality, however, can be something different. In fact, in the majority of the situations I have come across, the market knowledge was incomplete and in a few cases extremely inadequate.

It usually takes some prodding to establish the level of market knowledge in a marketing department. One of the key items to ascertain is whether the company has a very comprehensive market-map; the presence or absence of such a map is telling of a company's level of market know-how and awareness.

Acquiring a comprehensive market-map can take an extensive, and in some cases, an extraordinary amount of effort. A market-map analysis must be done in great detail, it must prove actionable, and it almost always points the way to large growth opportunities.

Surprisingly, I have found that without a map in place, people tend to imagine the market size they operate in to be smaller than it actually is. As a result, creating a map generates a huge amount of additional opportunities for existing products and services.

Now, what is a detailed market-map? What information does it provide? To my mind the "map" has in it a number of dimensions. It has the ability to

[1] I would like to acknowledge Professor Jonathan Frenzen and William J. Young Instructor, at the University of Chicago, Booth School of Business for input over the years on both this strategy and the strategy on sales force deployment; also implementation projects with Young and Associates, Ltd of Oak Brook, IL.

illustrate the total demand for the products or services and also identify exactly where the demand is. This analysis has to be done in enough detail so it can become actionable. In other words knowing that the total demand for a product is X is not good enough. You must also know how that demand is distributed geographically and be able to identify the customers and their size and address.

Because most companies look at figures that relate only to their own existing customers – not those customers they do not have, not to mention those they do not know even exist- it is not always easy to arrive at this information. But, it is exactly in these areas where the marketing effort is not sighted (i.e., the blind spots), where markets are out of easy view, that you will find the highest hidden value.

A market-map must also reveal your channels to market. While you need to be able to identify and understand these channels, as they are part of the market-map, it can be difficult to map them out and locate their relative size. If you are selling to someone who sells to someone else and thence to another party, either through resale of your product or incorporation into other products the situation becomes rather complex.

Nevertheless, as a rule, it is important to understand all the steps and, in particular, understand the dynamics of the ultimate and penultimate transactions. These last two transactions are the ones that will be the most influential on the demand of your products. Being able to influence them directly (not always possible) will add huge leverage to your business; the leverage will come both in terms of boosting demand and in the ability to introduce new products effectively.

Understanding and quantifying these areas sometimes can be achieved only with major effort; but this is why you will realize vast payback from ascertaining these factors. This understanding can lead to the total realignment and positioning of the sales and marketing effort and to some very strong permanent upside.

As a rule and also by way of a shortcut in the analysis, the closer to the end customer you can influence the sale of a product, the stronger your long-term position is.

Once you have applied the detailed mapping activity to your company, you must carry out the same assessments for your competitors and become familiar with the position they occupy on the market-map and in the channels to market. Clearly this information will have a bearing on your actions and will provide key considerations in the strategy selection to obtain advantage.

Yet another dimension, inherent in creating a market-map, is to understand market adjacencies. A market adjacency is a market that is closely aligned with yours but that does not directly intersect with yours. For instance, if you are in the market for men's sports apparel, an adjacency could be women's apparel. In an adjacency you generally can leverage and access many of the same assets, but you still need to do a lot of work to establish yourself in the new market, even in a situation as simple as the example in this paragraph.

After you have gathered data regarding market channels that exist for you and your competitors, you must become aware of how your market is likely to develop and in which direction it is likely to go. This awareness comes from understanding the dynamics in the market (including end demand and channels), the strengths of customers and competitors, and the latest technology. The largest prizes will come from the ability to read or forecast the shape of the market-map in the future before your competitors; the largest prize of all comes if you read the market and also use this data to establish the new market. The success of this approach is amply exemplified by a company like Apple® in what it has achieved the last few years with its robust moves to create and lead new markets.

If you are in the type of market where it is difficult to get a market-map, then you may have to invest major resources to obtain and maintain one, but it is well worth the effort and expense. This information will offer you significant competitive advantage precisely because it is very valuable and not easy to come by. An accurate market-map will enable you to be much more effective in your activities in the areas of marketing, in sales effort optimization and in achieving growth.

Strategy 6: Establish a Tailored Sales Force

There are few areas in business that are more misunderstood than sales force. There are also few areas in which it is more difficult to measure results and easier to obtain a highly unreliable and/or downright inaccurate reading. In reality, even if your sales are rising each year and even if your sales per sales person are rising each year as well, you cannot necessarily conclude from those figures alone that you are running a good sales force. It is also not necessarily correct to conclude that you are running a sales force geared to extract the maximum from the marketplace for its cost.

Of course, I advise that you cannot run a good sales force without an accurate market-map. Your map will tell you what sales potential exists in various areas, as well as the structure of your business channels. Your map helps you decide which channels to apply sales effort and to market more intensively. This mapping process precedes the sales effort redirection and makes the sales effort much more specific; in essence, the map is the basis for reprioritizing sales targets. You must define and target your sales efforts with respect to potential and not just with respect to history.

By putting all the items I have mentioned into play, you can increase the effectiveness of your sales force by between 50 to 100%. This rise is possible without even considering attention to other key activities, such as improving sales skills, expanding selling methodologies, updating training and introducing appropriate compensation plans.

In my experience, transforming a sagging sales force into a powerhouse is a long-term activity. Generally speaking, it requires at least two years of determined effort. You must develop the data and the tools, as well as implement the new direction before you begin realizing results. Even then, you are talking about a multiyear effort of continuous improvement. The reason the whole activity takes so long is that it involves many complex steps: you must first develop a market-map, then develop the marketing strategy, and finally determine the needed sales skills. After that, to achieve maximum effectiveness, you must retrain your sales force and assign new tasks to redeploy.

From a purely practical point of view, how do you assess where you are in your sales effort? You must begin by focusing your assessment efforts on two distinct, yet related, areas of sales: the quality of your sales people and your deployment methods.

When considering your sales force, you must ask yourself whether or not your sales people are effective, especially for your market. Markets can vary considerably and your sales people must be good matches for your market and its corresponding price points.

Then, too, although the skills and know-how needed for selling can be significantly different depending on the particular product, service and/or target market, when it comes to basic selling skills, there is commonality. Some people are good at it and others, despite all the training in the world, are just not cut out for it.

How do you determine whether or not you have a competent sales force? If sales is your own personal strength, you should accompany your sales people on sales calls. As you sit with them and observe their customer-selling skills in action, their level (or lack) of competence will soon become evident. If sales is not your strength, I recommend you hire experienced sales leaders who will be able to augment your observations and also become the trainers for a more effective sales force.

As for effective deployment, we must return to the market-map. Only if your company has a strong grasp of its market and a strong understanding of its channels to market with specificity and quantification (i.e., a clear market-map) will it experience a highly effective deployment process. This represents one of the largest upsides of putting such a map in place.

Clearly, what I am describing here is a process involving a heavy organizational change requiring patience as you wait for each step to work its magic. But eventually, I promise you will realize strong, staggering benefits. A powerful, well-run, targeted sales force provides a real competitive advantage and it is something that cannot be replicated by competitive entities overnight. Even if others attempt to replicate your success, you will usually maintain your lead if you execute continuous improvements on your end.

Strategy 7: Concentrate on High-Leverage Marketing Activities

Marketing is a vast and interesting subject encompassing many different activities. However, not all the activities have the same potential for impact. Effecting a transformation means finding the paths of highest impact. To produce the results you desire, I recommend you concentrate your systematic efforts in the four areas that follow.

A) Obtain optimum market price and optimum value for a given offering

Price is the most effective variable in the marketing mix and yet it is frequently ignored. I have often seen companies struggle with inadequate profitability for many years while giving customers full product value. This does not mean that these companies knew they missed the pricing lever or that they knew they missed the opportunity to do better. On the contrary, they were convinced that there was simply no room for them to secure a better price, only to discover (and I have seen this occur a number of times after an acquisition) that new management was able to obtain very large price increases. The income generated from these price increases most often turns marginal businesses into valuable ones.

Equally, understanding where your company has the ability to generate price is not easy. It requires strategic knowledge of the value its products bring to the market, detailed knowledge of how and where they are used and also detailed knowledge of substitutes. No effort to obtain more value from products or services will be successful without this type of understanding in place.

B) Understand the importance of the low end of the market

In most markets, market-share loss occurs because a competitor has entered the low end of the market. When this happens, companies that eventually fail are those willing to cede the low end under some notion that this is the only option to protect profitability. Before they know it, they are also ceding the middle of their market too, and soon find they have become marginalized.

The entry of a new competitor at the low end may signify a problem that goes well beyond mere pricing; it may also signify the existence of a major structural problem in the economics of the business or industry.

Whatever the reason, it is clear such activity cannot be dismissed or ignored. And yet, this mistake of ceding the low end occurs daily and causes many markets and market shares (from cars to electronics) to be handed over to new entrants. It is very damaging when companies are caught unprepared and do not have products and strategies waiting in the wings to protect the low end. Planning how you will protect the low end of your market and preparing for that time when a new entrant comes along should be a pivotal, perennial objective if you want to run a successful business. In addition, it will reveal opportunities you have with respect to your competitors and what action you must take to become the aggressor.

Please also note that the reason you may need a transformation today is that the low end has been ceded in the past. You cannot walk away from this problem. You have to face it head on as it may be the only path back to long-term viability.

C) Remain differentiated

One of the ways to ensure you stay differentiated is by introducing a continuous stream of new products, thus advancing constantly what is available in the market-place. By offering customers something new or by offering them a new pricing opportunity, you have much higher chances of success than if you fight it out with a me-too product. The only reason for a customer to switch to a me-too product (if he or she is happy with what he has in terms of quality and delivery) is price. You can, of course, win on price. But, if you embark on that strategy, you will need to establish the least-cost position long term and the means to remain there for a sufficient length of time, as others eventually will be able to match your cost position. Alternatively, others will simply sell their products for cash to survive as opposed to selling at economic reinvestment levels, thereby making the industry uneconomic.

D) Concentrate on activities designed to create new segments or generate new markets

To do this, you must identify and address new needs with new functionalities. While at first these activities may sound difficult, in practice they are not. In my experience, if you focus your organization on strong market understanding and innovation, and, interlace that effort with an entrepreneurial spirit, you will automatically generate initiatives that, in turn, will create new markets and segments.

The importance of creating new markets cannot be overstated, as for a period of time (perhaps a long time), you will have the sole offering in the marketplace. This provides you with the ability to capture new customers and sell them both your new and older products. The multiplier effect is huge. One strong, new offering that creates a new market or a new segment can become the cornerstone of a total business transformation.

··· Chapter 6 Main Points ···

1. Thoroughly understand and fine-tune the business model; do not assume you are already operating with an optimal model. Pay particular attention to how the change in model will affect the ability to supply differentiated products, acquire new customers and affect cost.

2. Systematically identify areas in which to concentrate investment and conversely to deemphasize it. Reallocation between the two is a major method of funding, and in a tight situation, probably the only one available.

3. Allocate new resources into the new areas with the most promising potential as opposed to the areas of strength of the past. The organization will automatically lead you to do the latter, something you need to avoid.

4. To find the best investment opportunities, spread understanding of investment basics throughout the whole of the organization; the use of simple payback concepts is recommended for this purpose.

5. A detailed market-map is essential and offers major advantage. It provides valuable insight regarding the size of the market, channels to market, the position of competitors and provides actionable data. Your map needs to lead to exploitation of areas not already served and of adjacencies; it also will assist your efforts to predict market direction.

6. Deploying effective sales coverage behind the market-map offers you a major competitive edge. It may require extensive reorientation of the scope and functioning of the sales force, but will result in a huge competitive advantage.

7. You gain extraordinary leverage if you develop strong marketing skills with regard to pricing, to covering systematically the low end of the market, to remaining differentiated and to creating your own markets and market segments.

········

CHAPTER 7 IN CONTEXT

Failing to Realize We Were Not Ready!

• • • • •

With any major initiative, you will find yourself pulled in two directions: You can never be rigorous and careful enough. But, on the other hand, you cannot paralyze yourself and never move forward.

By 2005, my Environmental and Combustion Controls management team and I were feeling very positive, and we were getting more and more daring. After all, in a mere three years we had transformed large parts of our business with clinical execution. We now developed products the marketplace loved and had established leading-edge manufacturing units. Customers wanted to buy from us again.

That February, at our national sales meeting, we launched a radical reorganization of the way we served the marketplace. The analysis supporting this initiative was overwhelming, and every indication showed that the project would offer superlative benefits.

Within a few weeks, there were indications that something had gone seriously wrong. While our first-line sales management still proclaimed we were on plan, they were the only ones. We let a few more weeks pass before key executive staff decided to travel with different salespeople around the country to find out what was really happening.

It did not take long to figure out we had a sizeable screw-up on our hands that had effectively paralyzed the organization! We thought we had put the basics in place, but we had not done so:

- *Roles, duties and expectations were not clear.*

- *The suitability of different personnel and personnel selection for new roles was not optimal.*

- *People in new roles had inadequate training.*

- *We had no clear metrics in terms of sales calls and achievements during them.*

- *There were no clear operating mechanisms.*

- *We launched with an incomplete computer system and database support for the new organization.*

In retrospect, it was easy to question why we had not piloted this effort in just a single region instead of launching nationally and involving hundreds of people. But questions like this would not help us now.

At this point, we could not go backwards. We had to fix what we had created and put it back on track. The effort to do this consumed a sizeable part of our company resources the rest of the year, and we did eventually get it right and maintained our growth path for the year. For subsequent years this turned out to be a "game-changing" initiative.

But it was important to recognize that our execution caused a major risk to the business. It was one that we mitigated only because we had the systems and the culture to recognize our errors, set our pride aside and work with our people up and down the organization to fix them. Had we managed to foresee we were not ready to launch, we would have avoided a lot of additional work, disruption and unnecessary risk to the business.

CHAPTER **7**

Risk Balancing and Inside Out Sequencing

Chapter Overview

This chapter aims to raise awareness of risk issues, and in particular the types of everyday risks that naturally exist in companies in need of transformation. It discusses the risks in the plans associated with such companies. The discussion is aimed at developing a robust transformation strategy at lower risk; this is achieved by fixing fundamentals and basics and developing core competencies as precursors and enablers to success. The discussion centers on risk arising from both the organization and business standpoints.

What Is Risk?

In an environment of recent financial collapses and diminutions of most people's assets, the word risk assumes a special, personal, even poignant meaning. A plan was established by many individuals and an expectation was created but the outcome did not match that expectation.

There are many investors today who feel totally misled and horribly let down by the guys who professed they were experts. Professionals in the financial field, who got swept up in the tide, might also look back at the situation and kick themselves for not seeing the impending watershed. And those professionals who did some of the complex mathematical calculations to prove that there was no risk out there, and therefore believed more investments should be made, might even be conflicted on how mathematical logic could be wrong. Before things went awry, and as markets were rising, these very same individuals were probably congratulating themselves on their wisdom, foresight and investment prowess.

So what happened? During the time prior to the collapse were they not running risks? Or did risk somehow not exist during that time period? The fact is that immediately before the "watershed events" the risk was at its highest but the expectation and visibility of that risk were at their lowest! In retrospect (and hindsight is always perfect) a lot of the assumptions were flawed or downright incorrect.

Now, I know there have been enough books and doctoral theses written on the subject of risk to fill a multitude of libraries. But, being that this is a practical book meant to serve as an aid to the everyday businessperson, I must define risk very simply. I must also define it simply for my own edification; otherwise, I may not be able to remember or recognize it or might become too confused to address it when it looms most dangerously. I define risk as the difference between expectation of an outcome and what actually happens.

Now the word expectation is very complex, as it arises from knowledge, facts and personal makeup. In addition risk becomes mitigated or multiplied within the interaction of all these elements. Expectation usually embodies a range of outcomes and is often not limited to one single point.

How Does Risk Arise and How Can You Mitigate It?

If risk represents the difference between expectation of an outcome and what actually happens, we can theoretically build a series of tools to assess the risk and ideally mitigate it. While it is true that not all risk can be assessed or mitigated (and the chapter end offers more discussion on this), this chapter generates awareness for the part of the risk that you can recognize and mitigate up-front.

Expectation always originates with an individual, and if that individual is not knowledgeable, there automatically exists a high level of risk. Now this statement may sound basic but it is remarkable how many decisions are made by two people who reinforce each other's beliefs, when in fact neither one understands the subject they are discussing!

Then again, let's examine the extreme cases of Mr. New and Mr. Longstanding (from Chapter 3) as viewed with the lens of risk. From day one, just by stepping into a new environment, Mr. New represents a large risk to his enterprise. Unless Mr. New is aware of the risk and how to mitigate it, he will surely make major errors. At the same time Mr. Longstanding may also represent high risk, especially if he does not fundamentally question and understand the way decisions and operations occur in the firm and how they should change over time. In other words, on a practical level, risk mitigation begins with understanding personal limitations and the environment you are in.

I do not have a magic solution for lack of knowledge but I can offer a remedy: to develop the instinct to know when you do not know. In addition, you must address lack of knowledge so that decision-making becomes informed and secure.

Like any new incumbent, Mr. New must transfer and digest a vast amount of information before he can make quality business decisions. He needs to acquire knowledge related to internal matters, people and assets. Then, too, he must acquire knowledge related to the industry, industry structure, industry economics and competition. In Chapter 4 we discussed the need for an operating mechanism. The Business Decision Week operating mechanism I describe and recommend is not only ideal for helping Mr. New get up to speed fast and assess the risks lurking in the business, it also helps mitigate the risk that comes from placing a newcomer in charge.

BDW imposes a rhythm on the business, and the issues (generally of the same nature) appear and reappear and are progressed from meeting to meeting. Besides affording the opportunity of a very steep learning curve, it offers a strong appreciation of the risks involved! Adoption of the techniques mentioned in Chapter 5 on enhanced decision-making such as openness, visibility, forward thinking and allowing for gestation time are also geared exactly to the issue of reducing risk. So are the adoption of effective processes and culture.

Ultimately, a lot of risk is mitigated, from a knowledge point of view, by becoming a subject-matter expert, knowing when you do not know and recognizing when the available knowledge and data are insufficient. Then again, even if you and others believe you are subject-matter experts, it is not always sufficient as extraordinary events can happen that shake the foundations of assumptions. This is where judgment and that "sixth sense" come in, both unquantifiable and essential in terms of decision-making.

While this chapter is not about expected value analysis, such analysis is a very useful tool to have in your back pocket. In most business situations the outcome will not be totally predictable. That is why it can be very beneficial to spread in an organization a couple of simple ideas: First, what is the range of outcomes foreseen if matters go well and if matters go badly? Second, what is the best and what is the worst outcome, and what is the range in between?

The expected value is the probability-weighted mean but in most practical situations it is a very insufficient guide. For secure outcomes you do not need only the mean, but the variance around the mean to be in a good place with a very little chance of significantly worse outcomes on the downside; the probability of the upside can be as wide as it can be!

I gave a coherent example in this sort of thinking in my commodity-buying discussion in Chapter 5. Any decision has inherently an upside and a downside. Personally, I stay away from decisions that hold potential for catastrophic downsides (no matter the lure of the upside). I also stay away from endeavors where the mean is not comfortably situated above an acceptable minimum, thus offering a wide margin for error.

Organizational Competence and Learning How to "Crawl"

Unfortunately knowledge and intellectual understanding alone, although a necessary start, are not sufficient to eliminate risk. Most decisions, projects and activities will need to be carried out by a large number of people. Clear direction helps; however, every day there will be twists and turns, and the necessary organizational competence needs to be in place so you and others can make the next-level decisions and carry them to execution.

I have remarked before that organizations in need of transformation are in trouble on a number of levels. Beyond lacking confidence they may have lost key competencies in critical areas, they may have lost key personnel (particularly people with essential subject-matter knowledge), they may have lost key leadership and they may not possess decision-making basics.

Equally, organizations which have gone through a fast expansion, without the necessary training, culture, processes and controls, may also run into a lot of the same issues.

Keen observation is the major tool for assessing the state of your organizational competence. Before trusting your organization with situations putting a lot at risk, you need to form a judgment regarding the key competencies of the organization and its capability to execute. To form this judgment, you have to rely on what you find out in talking to key people as well as examine the recent achievements of the organization.

In assessing the competence of an organization, it is prudent to triangulate major decisions from many aspects. Let me give you an illustrative example because I have observed quite frequently that the guys with the least ability to execute, have the most optimistic views about time scales for achieving results, about the costs involved and about the magnitude of the results to be obtained. They also have the poorest appreciation of the inherent risks.

I was meeting with colleagues to review a proposal to spend major capital to upgrade one of our facilities. Being new to the business I was extremely impressed by the quality of the presentation and the fluency and use of a number of buzz words I had not heard before. Being a cautious guy I asked about the history of similar projects at the same site. Other than offering me additional assurances of guaranteed success, my colleagues became rather reticent on the topic.

This sent up a red flag for me; I kept probing and in the end I requested a full review of the projects undertaken the last five years at the site. Those reviews revealed that none of the multimillion-dollar projects we had undertaken in the time period had met objectives. In effect we were not really doing well for all the money spent. So what was wrong here? What of the rhetoric and the terrific PowerPoint® presentation?

Upon further examination, I discovered we were failing at a number of different levels including leadership, business acumen and technical understanding, and we had a major deficiency in our ability to execute. This is the multiple-mode failure I alluded to earlier and it cannot be remedied overnight. The only strategy available is to start fixing, and if you are patient, persistent and demanding you will be able to get to the necessary level of competence in a few quarters.

As for my example on previous page we never proceeded with the proposed project. In retrospect it was ill conceived and, had we moved forward with it, it would have become an unprofitable investment. We lacked the fundamental understanding and the competence necessary to be successful. Instead we concentrated our efforts on improving our fundamentals.

When you have whole groups of good people deluding themselves as to where they stand in their understanding, and in what it takes to make the right calls and deliver, then there are indeed some gigantic gaps between expectation and result. That is the basic definition of risk. This is why I believe that the operating mechanism has to be employed to systematically assess and transform the business, cycle after cycle, while simultaneously enhancing the basic thinking and competences. This is what reduces risk.

I find it helpful to initiate projects and tasks for the purpose of testing the level of understanding and ability to execute. These are the kind of projects that will not break the bank. Rather they are projects that will show the real state of competence and form the basis for mentoring and for finding what the inadequacies are. Again the constancy of the BDW operating mechanism and its ability to mold a team and offer a forum for exchanging ideas and solidifying plans is of great help. It absolutely guarantees that from month to month you will realize a visible improvement in competence. And, as competence increases, risk decreases.

Before you start undertaking major (risky) projects and as a further step in risk reduction, you must undertake systematic identification of gaps and deficiencies. These gaps can be closed by a combination of methods that include the right know-how, the right players, the right systems and the right controls. To reduce risk in a transformation you need to have the skill set to identify where the gaps are and the systematic approach to put the fundamentals in place to close them ahead of major initiatives.

This could mean that you may have to pass up on a lot of opportunities and projects until you know you have closed those gaps and are treading on solid ground. This can be frustrating and requires discipline, but it leads to success!

For example, you may find you have to pass on a great acquisition because your company lacks good processes to run itself and execute such a project; you may have to delay investments that appear to make sense because you are not convinced you can execute well; you may be unable to expand a sales effort because you do not have a good market-map, etc. But the key approach is that, if these activities are going to be important to your organization, you have to put in place the capabilities they require in advance so you can execute at low risk and at higher probability of success.

It is great to observe steady progress and a rising level of competence within an organization. Such a "learning how to crawl" approach functions as a prelude to walking and then sprinting.

Are You Ready to Execute Without Undue Risk?

To be sure, we are in business to take on risk, but I never advise taking on undue risk.

What qualifies as undue risk? On the internal side, undue risk is present when your business:

- Has not built up the methodologies and common language of communication and processes.

- Does not have the rigor in its decision-making and is unable to rank opportunities and define the next best alternative.

- Operates in the absence of robust metrics and lacks well-understood processes over the life of the project, thus preventing deviations and required changes from being detected and addressed in a timely fashion.

- Lacks subject-matter experts and the knowledge base is not as comprehensive as it needs to be.

- Applies business models to situations where they are not relevant.

- Does not understand the markets in great depth and does not have a detailed market-map in place.

- Lacks a good grasp of technology trends.

Because there are many risk-related factors you cannot control, you cannot expect to be able to mitigate all risks. Markets change, demand changes and competitive landscape changes, and while these items are generally not in our control, they are a large part of the decision mix. On the other hand, a well-run company that is able to become the leader in its marketplace can actually mitigate some of this external risk too. This is because it is the one dictating the pace and the changes in the marketplace and the competition must react to it. There is a big difference between leading and reacting, and the business leader's risk profile is generally lower than that of the companies trying to keep up.

When it comes to risk factors, I like to build an organizational capability designed to eliminate undue risk to the fullest extent possible. I liken the process to building a machine that delivers robust execution on key projects and initiatives with enough visibility to avoid dead ends. And I go further than that. Before spending huge amounts of money (huge being a relative term that depends on the situation you are leading) I test-run the machine, making sure it is up to the task at hand and that it can undertake bigger and bigger tasks.

A Systematic Approach to Mitigate Risk

This section brings together all the considerations mentioned so far in this chapter and sets out the systematic, practical steps for combating and reducing risk in most situations. Depending on your situation, some of the steps can be skipped, but bear in mind that a systematic approach does enhance success.

Step 1: Fix your fundamentals

My first concern in running a business is to fortify the areas that constitute the biggest danger, namely the areas of internal fundamentals. Fundamentals appear simple but, in reality, even successful organizations may have significant deficiencies in these areas. Alternatively, the deficiencies become disabling in a major economic recession or when competition becomes tougher.

Your company may not be hemorrhaging now, but, as a preventive measure against future disasters, check to see if you have adequate methodologies at work in your basics, such as inventories, receivables, information systems and customer service. You must ask yourself: are we paying enough attention to the fundamentals? Do our fundamentals pose an immediate risk? Are our fundamentals negatively affecting cash flow? Are we prepared to withstand a major change in demand or a major recession?

Of course, none of these items will, in and of themselves, break your business when the going is easy, but under conditions of stress (such as a recession or entry of a tough competitor) they can certainly do that. In addition if they are not securely in place you are leaving a lot of opportunity on the table and so you must work to get them there.

Step 2: Face up to areas of competitive weakness

This step must take place concurrently with your examination of fundamentals and looks externally. Entrenched competitive weakness shows in the sales statistics. Are you seeing in your sales statistics losses that reflect diminished competitiveness? Are your sales people reporting that competition has superior products and generally your win/loss ratio is not advantageous? Is this a sales and marketing execution problem, or is it a lack of new product problem? Is it a lack of adequate R&D pipeline problem? Is this a fundamental cost problem or pricing power problem? Please note that competitive weakness is the sort of problem that, if allowed to persist can really bury a company. Again, in a weak company all these shortcomings may be there as well as many more.

Although you may not be able to fix all of these weaknesses at once, and the fixes will be time consuming, you need to attack the problem immediately and establish a clear priority of what you will attack first. In many situations you will have to fix competitiveness issues while also fixing fundamentals, as neither activity can wait. All these activities will require putting the right people in place to address the problems, making available the right resources, directing, coaching, encouraging, goading, pushing, shoving and providing vision and encouragement to get results.

In my experience, a few correct initiatives, done really well, go a long way! They also serve as a visible example to an organization of what can be achieved; the organization sees what the expectations are, the "juices" begin flowing, and the bar is raised…and raised.

Step 3: Identify and avoid potential accidents

In a transformation, you will be guiding your company into a new direction and driving it forward faster than it has ever been driven before. In consequence, a lot of areas, if not adequate today, will soon be found even more wanting. You need to identify these areas of current and future weakness on a systematic basis and improve them ahead of time to avoid accidents. Nothing destroys value as needlessly as accidents. Accidents do not happen out of the blue; they happen because you did not predict them and because you did not know how to avoid them. They require an annoyingly large amount of time to fix and can really railroad your transformation process.

Let me give you two examples of avoidable accidents. First, let's say you are about to introduce a new technology. Let's imagine you do not really know how to test this new technology because historically your company did not have in place the necessary people, equipment, know-how and procedures for such extensive testing. So, in essence, you are really exposed. Instead of holding back and waiting until you have put the proper capabilities in place, you proceed and launch the product at great expense and with great fanfare only to find out that the technology is not fully proven. As a result, you experience a major recall and a loss of reputation for many years. This is the type of major accident you could really do without!

As a second example, let's say you have become bedazzled by a well-presented investment bank acquisition presentation. Let's pretend you get into a bidding contest and wind up buying something at unrealistic assumptions and for an uneconomic price. Now this is again a major accident you will have to live with for many years to come. You would be much wiser to develop the core competencies and reflexes necessary to absolutely avoid these sorts of accidents.

Step 4: Introduce tomorrow's needed capabilities in advance

If you are avoiding big risks and if you are out there finding low-hanging fruit and fixing fundamentals does it mean you have no strategic aim? Are you just going through your quarters, improving operations and hoping for the best? The answer is no, especially if you intend to transform a company as opposed to just make it more efficient! The issue is that to transform a company you need to develop new capabilities, and this is the perfect time to start developing these–while you are fixing the fundamentals.

Ideally, you need to be putting in place the core competencies that you will need in the next steps of your transformation. Putting these in place will make for faster and less risky execution as you begin to step out into new areas. The sooner you can identify strategic direction the better off you are, as the strategic path is the optimal place to add enabling capabilities. But you need to choose. I have seen managers drive their organizations by branching out in all sorts of directions without consistency or theme; in the end they achieve very little. Worse, in the process, they unwittingly increase the risk profile of the operation.

If you have not yet chosen a strategic direction, a very good concurrent activity is to get a number of hypotheses for a strategic framework in place and then proceed to test; the best test is real activity in the marketplace. In the meantime, you can use the time to set in place capabilities that are bound to become useful in the future (when you are ready to pull the trigger). Such preliminary capability-building areas may include knowledge related to

- Establishing plants in new geographies

- Marketing in a different channel

- Expanding product development and technology capabilities in markets in which you are not currently strong

- Investing in key enabling assets and equipment

To reduce future risk, you must take these steps in advance of the actual initiatives.

I do understand there are specific circumstances, such as when a business is caving in on itself, where the formula of working on the low-risk activities first, fixing fundamentals and developing core competencies ahead of major strategic moves does not appear feasible. Although I cannot preclude the possibility that this is the case, my response to this is threefold.

First, if a company is that close to terminal, there is no point getting into it if you are an outsider. Second, if this is a business you have been running for a long time, then if you had adopted some of the techniques advocated in this book, you would have seen the situation coming a lot earlier and would have had time to do something about it before it became terminal. Third—and this is what I genuinely believe—even if you are in the center of a business storm, but you have an eye that sees, you will find solutions to problems that are relatively low risk and sustainable.

The Inside Out Strategy

Finding and establishing a new, long-term direction is clearly a key requirement in a transformation journey; it is of paramount importance. However, it is also important to have the right level of expectation of when and how this new, more effective, long-term direction will be found!

At the outset you may set up a few initiatives or a few investigative efforts specific to identifying long-term direction. But in reality, if you have walked into a company that is in a bad strategic position (or you are running one where performance is deteriorating), the best thing you can do is to immerse yourself in the company and its marketplace with an open mind and a fresh eye. Let facts and situations soak in and let those big, ah-ha moments (major, consequential observations) hit you between the eyes. It has often been said that the greatest value comes from something you do not expect, so let serendipity do some work as well!

Clearly, the earlier you can begin to identify the long-term direction and verify it month by month, the better off you are going to be. It may take a while to find the right direction, or it may just be staring you in the face. If you are facing a severe competitiveness problem you need to start attacking aspects of that immediately and establish solutions; this is irrespective of the long-term direction! All solutions begin with doing preliminary scoping work and putting in place, step by step, the right people and assets to begin to execute. Please note that frequently, in addressing a severe competitiveness problem, you also may find a large component of the long-term strategy.

It is because finding and verifying long-term direction is so consequential and time consuming that I advocate that the strategy has to be an inside out one. In other words, if you want to improve a company you need to begin by looking at your processes and move fast to make them robust. This applies whether you are familiar with the business or not. You need to fine-tune and improve capabilities in these areas. You need to increase performance and lower cost. You need to develop and put in place the systems that will enable growth. You need to put in place the productivity actions that will provide the cash for the growth activities. This is a process involving investment reallocation and effort redirection.

In parallel, you need to investigate the long-term direction you will follow. When you have attained the desired level of confidence and verification, you can begin to invest with certainty in new areas and initiatives that entail higher risk.

This is where I differ in my approach from the orthodoxy of "strategic moves first." To my mind this approach can be suboptimal and foolhardy; it certainly can be a play of lower probability of success. Strategic moves take time to mature and develop; there is no point in trying to force them into an unworkable time frame or in committing the company to a new direction prematurely. By the same token, trying to embark on a new strategic direction before the fundamentals are in place unnecessarily multiplies the risk and increases the chances of failure.

So how long do you concentrate primarily on the inside and "scout" the outside? In my experience it takes a minimum of 12 months, and may take closer to 24 months, to put in the operating mechanism and effect sufficient internal changes, to create momentum and have a robust platform to work with. Clearly, this depends on the size of the enterprise and how broken the starting point was to begin with.

To me the inside out (fix fundamentals first) approach offers a huge springboard for success. It gets you ready to really transform the company without incurring undue risk. On the contrary, you have strengthened your business and improved your probability of success in all respects.

· · · Chapter 7 Main Points · · ·

1. In a simple definition, risk is the difference between expectation and what actually occurs. Being cognizant of personal lack of knowledge improves outcomes, as does having real subject-matter experts on your team.

2. Getting your organization into the habit of thinking in terms of range of outcomes, as opposed to a single point, and implementing activities with generous margins of error assists in your success.

3. Weak businesses have failures at multiple levels. To reduce the risk, you need to methodically identify the gaps and close them. This may take a long time during which you must train your organization how to crawl.

4. You need to get your company to the point of executing without undue internal and external risk. Undue risk arises from a lot of simple areas, such as lack of common language of communication, lack of everyday decision-making skills and lack of market understanding.

5. While you build your organizational capability select low-risk initiatives. Such initiatives have fast payback, and involve a lot of the free levers mentioned in Chapter 1 and the seven strategies in Chapter 6.

6. A good generic approach is to fix the fundamentals first, face up to areas of competitive weakness, identify and avoid potential accidents and introduce in advance those capabilities that will be needed later on.

7. The inside out strategy suggests that it is optimal for you to fix and enhance the core fundamentals first. This provides the time you need to identify and test major strategic moves and provides the robust capability you will need to carry them out. This results in substantially higher probabilities of success when placing large bets.

· · · · ● · · · ·

CHAPTER 8 IN CONTEXT
Learning to Identify Game-Changing Moves

• • • • •

Specialty Additives is a global business within Honeywell Specialty Materials; it has some unique fundamental technologies and the ability to customize these technologies to more than 1,000 applications. Materials from this business are used in floor polish, lipstick, automotive coatings, coatings for fresh fruit, the manufacture of textiles and plastic pipes, and sunscreen ...just to name a few.

Specialty Additives has long been a terrific growth business. For the two years prior to 2008 and the recessionary environment, it grew its volumes by some 15%. This was the situation when the team presented to me at my first Business Decision Week as CEO of Specialty Materials in April 2008.

The more I listened, the more I was impressed ... the growth story sounded terrific. Of course, it was hard not to conclude that with all these potential markets that something might be missing – there should be more opportunity to this business.

I congratulated the team and told them given the vastness of the applications of these technologies it should be possible to do even more. In particular, if we looked at our markets deeply enough, we should be able to find some "game-changing" applications leading to new businesses.

The team had been in place for several years, and they were not used to this type of feedback. Usually, they had been praised for their growth rates, not pushed to come up with game-changers. Visibly, they were less than pleased with my comments.

To their credit, they came back to Business Decision Week in 30 days saying they felt that the first step was to improve the methods they had of looking at multiple markets and customer requests (they were handling over 500 at the time) and to invest in new global systems to manage the effort, to which I agreed.

Within three months, the Specialty Additives team came back with some potential game-changing opportunities. One in particular caught my attention.

If you have ever seen roads being surfaced, you have seen the steaming trucks loaded with asphalt. Because of the way it is formulated, the asphalt has to be laid down at very high temperatures. Our technologists felt they could use our additives to enable the paving of a better road surface at significantly lower temperatures – about 75°F by their early calculations. This would save vast amounts of energy globally, reduce greenhouse gas emissions and really add value. Just think, there are more than 12 million miles of roads in the U.S., European Union, India and China, the vast majority of which are paved. And think of all the roads that are being built today, especially in emerging regions. Wow – talk about a market opportunity!

With a recession under way, the team cautiously asked that we hire a person to begin exploring further. Well, this is not the type of idea you hold back on, even during a recession. I asked them to start with five people. Within 18 months, we had people in a new vertical market involved in paving roads in 5 U.S. states, China and a couple of European countries. Clearly, this is a business that can grow for a long time.

This team now understood very well the concept of game-changing initiatives and put it to diligent work. Between 2008 and 2010, as a lot of their traditional markets contracted, Specialty Additives entered multiple new applications and geographies to increase profitability by another 60 percent ...through the worst recession in 70 years!

CHAPTER **8**

Finding the Game-Changing Moves

Chapter Overview

Game-changing moves deliver differentiation in the marketplace and provide above market growth. As such, they modify the course of a business and deliver breakout potential.

Finding and initiating game-changing moves is not a trivial undertaking. This chapter establishes considerations for identifying game-changing moves and illustrates the link between such moves and relevant core capabilities. In addition, it discusses the need for decisive, timely programs that help establish such moves and argues against relying solely on cost as a differentiator. Here you will discover arguments and examples demonstrating how game-changing moves generally emanate from understandings related to market or technology, with the most powerful moves representing a combination of the two.

Game-Changing Moves Can Make You (and Their Absence Can Break You)

By definition, a game-changing move is an initiative that helps reposition a business in the marketplace and confers it market advantage. Such initiatives include those that:

- Give an organization the prospect of growth of a few percentage points above market growth rates.

- Forestall the decline of the sales line, especially when market or technology conditions shift adversely, forcing the company into a corner.

- Lead a company to permanently break out of a rut of stagnating or declining margins.

- Preserve long-term competitiveness in light of shifting global markets.

- Latch onto technological shifts and market shifts early.

- Move into market adjacencies or invent new markets.

- Expand global reach and perform better in high-growth (emerging) markets.

Note that a game-changing initiative must have a strong market and growth component to it and not rely on cost alone. As discussed later on in this chapter, it is rare for an initiative that solely enables cost advantage can also be sustainable and unique enough to qualify as a game-changing move.

The above list is not exhaustive but the theme is one of a consequential initiative to expand competitiveness and provide profitable, above-market growth. There is also a defensive element in this whole concept. If we go back to the table in Chapter 1, I believe a certain degree of growth (above 5%) is required as a minimum to ensure satisfactory profitability (double-digit earnings growth). If the market you are in is not growing that fast, the only way to get to satisfactory returns is by initiating or inventing game-changing moves.

Inertia Is the Enemy of Game-Changing Moves

By definition, an initiative requires stepping out and doing something different. Some individuals are predisposed towards new initiatives; these are the people who get up every morning and want to identify something new and work out how they will take advantage of it. These are the disciplined, well-organized managers who understand the importance of balancing day-to-day responsibilities with making time to identify, investigate and initiate new projects and new ideas.

But, carving out enough time to identify new initiatives is only the first challenge; another is organizational inertia, as most people naturally resist anything that involves new learning and new ways. It may be hard for them to perceive and understand the importance of the change and even harder for them to work out what to do and acclimate to new work methods and routines. It is not easy to step out of a routine. Routines can be dull and predictable, but they are also comfortable. It is for this reason that new ideas require a high level of effort to be defined and launched before they gain a momentum of their own. The definition and initial launch phase require systematic, day-to-day management and caretaking if the young ideas are to take hold, survive and thrive.

Considerations for Identifying Game-Changing Moves

If you are prospecting for oil or gold, most likely you have done significant homework on identifying the kind of geology that might contain these minerals. If you are smart, you do not go around sinking holes all over the place on a random basis. You have some preconceived ideas, models and science.

Finding game-changing moves is not much different from prospecting. You need to know where to look; you also have to be prepared to cut your losses early and move on if your efforts are not meeting the necessary success potential.

The degree of difficulty in finding a winning move varies with the circumstances. In a few circumstances (and you should be able to spot these from a mile away) it is next to impossible to find a winning move. This could happen, for instance, when a total market or technology disappears or becomes obsolete overnight taking your company along with it. Unless you saw the danger looming and put in place the steps to be part of the changing landscape, it may be too late to react in a contracting, terminal market. But as we are discussing here, good management is about creating solutions ahead of problems.

It is rare that a single game-changing move will solve all your problems by providing the required growth rates, by offering competitive advantage and/or by safeguarding profitability. In practice, you need to identify and test a number of initiatives, knowing ahead of time that some will not pan out. For items that no longer look promising, you will want to develop the discipline of cutting losses early before commitments become large. It is also desirable to have a handful of potential game-changing moves available for the sake of diversification. But beware: taking on too many initiatives can lead to dilution of financial and human resources, so you will want to strike a healthy balance between too few initiatives and attempting too many as both scenarios can lead to achieving too little.

It is also worth noting that because of the way competition behaves in some industries, maintaining a steady performance—especially in areas where competitors make severe errors or take on outlandish risks—can be sufficient to succeed. For this reason, I do not believe that anyone should miss an opportunity to meet competitors and understand their motivation and capabilities. The act of meeting competitors and industry leaders is something that must take place within an appropriate context and well within a legal framework with regard to competition. But, I find that ordinary social discussions about family or sport or background still provide valuable insights.

To my mind, if you are looking for strong moves there is no substitute for sensitizing the whole of an organization to be alert to new opportunities. You can discover large opportunities in the marketplace and in new technologies; but the largest of all are found within a combination of the two, as when a new technology enables the creation of a new market or superior products. But whatever the genesis of the opportunity, the end result must be a new initiative that will provide access to or create new markets; alternatively this initiative will provide a deeper penetration of current markets as well as higher sales growth.

Whenever you identify new game-changing moves, it is worth quantifying what they could mean in terms of sales. Although this is not always possible to do with accuracy, you need to know in advance if there is sufficient upside. Even better is an initial vision that reveals an upside while hinting of more to come after that.

Preserve and Build Well-Placed Capabilities

When management relies on indiscriminate cost cutting as a solution, it can be because it does not see the necessity for game-changing moves or it does not understand the connection between core capabilities and game-changing moves. This lack of awareness manifests itself in actions that are deeply flawed and that serve to disable the company's ability to compete in the marketplace. Here is an example from my experience.

I had taken a new position and within the first week on the job, I was presented with two decisions. These decisions came my way as a courtesy, as they were practically ready to be implemented. Both decisions featured cost reduction as motivation. As it turned out, well-meaning people were trying to tackle issues beyond their understanding and were simply carrying out what they perceived was company policy. At the time, prevailing thinking said that anything having to do with cost reduction was a good thing, especially if you could find some clever, vaguely plausible reason to justify it.

The two propositions were very explicit. The first one indicated that a substantial part of our engineering would simply be let go from the United States and substituted with some lower-cost engineers from the Far East. The second proposition was equally simple: we would fire the customer support we had in place in various countries around Europe and substitute it with one lower-cost support center in a single country.

On paper both these decisions sounded great and proclaimed very attractive financial projections. But, upon more careful consideration, they were fundamentally flawed as they destroyed some key capabilities.

As I considered the first situation, I wondered why on earth would we replace thousands of man-years of knowledge in engineering specific to our products with people who were essentially "green" and who would need the equivalent amount of training to learn? This initiative made no sense to me and, to the dismay of its advocates, I cancelled it.

As an epilogue to this story, a few months later a chill went through me when I realized that had I agreed to this decision, it would not have been possible to transform the company and lead it to better days. The engineering capability was excellent, and eventually it became a cornerstone of our recovery and was the bedrock of a major game-changing move. In contrast, it was our general-management thinking that was lacking in clarity and our product managers who did not know how to leverage this great asset. That is not to say that we did not go on to establish engineering in Asia anyway, but this was in the context of a coherent strategy that called for the establishment of further core capabilities to help us perform better in those markets and globally.

The second proposition—the one that advocated cutting support in local European countries and concentrating instead on just one country—could only have come from people of limited international experience. The proposition of removing in-country European support was fundamentally flawed. Our customer base did not consist of large, sophisticated customers; they were small businesses owned and run by people who wanted to be serviced locally in their own language and not in English. Again, I refused to go along with the scheme of consolidating these support centers into a single, English-speaking location.

We did not have the monopoly in bad ideas. In fact, as is true in the fashion industry, management fads do seem to sweep through corporations. Another company in a similar market did follow through with this ill-conceived plan of removing local support. I watched with interest and within 18 months its business in Europe literally imploded. This put a huge amount of financial stress on the parent company with large loss of profitability and precipitated a multiyear contraction.

After suffering a catastrophic event like that, the road to recovery is long and hard; this is because years of relationships and of presence in the marketplace are lost. In contrast, we maintained our local European capabilities and over time made them more efficient and more effective at serving the right customers. The latter formula worked, and it worked well.

If you are thinking the situations I described above are unique, they are not. It is surprising how many executives I have known who told me, with gleaming eyes, how they would earn huge amounts of money by outsourcing their business to some low-cost supplier on another continent. What they were not able to visualize were tomorrow's dynamics. Very soon, without internal capability, they found themselves in the hands of the supplier who, sooner or later, put other people in the business or entered the end market directly himself or simply raised prices and extracted all the available profit. Naiveté rules eternal!

While it is easy to destroy capability, it is far more difficult to create or rebuild the same. It is especially hard work to set up capability for new initiatives. First, you do not quite know what you are looking for and second, this is something totally new. So you have a chicken and egg situation of not having a sure path of knowing how to find a beginning. The key to success lies in defining sufficiently the value proposition, then locating the right person or persons to lead those activities that will refine the initiative and establish the foundational work.

Procrastination Increases Cost; Fast Action Saves Cost

In some situations you have an urgent need to find game-changing moves. Perhaps these situations are close to my mind because I have been exposed to companies in immediate need of transformation.

From experience, I have seen what can happen when individuals do not hold a serious regard for potential loss of competitiveness or emerging threats. I have also known those who believe that what exists now will remain in place forever and they are under no threat. In either case, as these individuals sense no immediate danger, they tend to accept the status quo and put off taking any action at all.

But procrastination is no solution. For one thing, procrastination escalates the cost and difficulty of game-changing; the later you take countermeasures, the lengthier and more difficult they are to execute and the more expensive the solution becomes. Conversely, the quicker you react to staunch a problem or exploit a new opportunity, the higher the chances of success. Of course, there is a fine line between running scared and being alert to potential threats and evaluating them continuously. However, it always pays to remain vigilant because whether you are reacting to a competitive problem or reaching for new opportunity, early action brings benefits.

While the above may appear self evident, it is lamentable, and at times downright bizarre, to witness the spectacle of companies both large and small that are somehow blind to these obvious principles.

In 2008, we witnessed the bankruptcy of a large part of the American Motor Industry. Much had been made of the predicament the Industry found itself in—a predicament that was totally predictable and only a matter of time. Many point to union issues and the uneconomic agreements made some 40 years earlier. On the other hand, I do not believe enough attention has been paid to other blunders and sheer lack of understanding of events in the marketplace. Year after year, the companies continued to put out low-quality products that were unattractive and lacking in basic features. During most of this time period these companies possessed vast resources and technology capabilities equal to or higher than their competitors; these resources and capabilities could have more than addressed these issues.

Instead, they ceded the low-end market (a cardinal marketing strategy error because young consumers begin at the low-end and generally migrate to more upscale, profitable cars within the same brand), never addressed quality and kept producing a plethora of mediocrity, none offering sufficient economies of scale. Competition invested much less capital in its factories (did not go on a crazy automation drives) and, under lean methodologies, used human resources effectively. Competition's strategy to concentrate behind a few models and product quality resulted in model volumes that offered constant recovery of the investment that in turn, enabled continual product upgrading. The latter provides reason for people to come and buy, thus reinforcing the growth in sales and accelerating the next introductions.

What I have just described here amounts to game-changing moves by competition, made more effective by three decades' worth of lack of appropriate response from the incumbents. At any point in time, the incumbents could have broken this vicious cycle by directing wasted resources into areas specifically meant to improve their business' fundamentals.

Please note that the above requires some of the methodologies already discussed in this book: reallocating resources to the areas that need to be fixed and improved, removal of investment from areas that do not return money, concentration on fixing the key fundamentals that become enablers, and developing those key capabilities that make the difference and that enable effective competition.

It is indicative of the cost of losing customers that a few years before the bankruptcies, the quality of American manufacturers' products did improve, but once you lose a customer, it is not so easy to get him or her back. To win a customer back, you need to demonstrate a wide margin of superiority over the new incumbents—a tough task indeed! This fact suggests that, as an executive, you need to do everything you can in an urgent fashion to stop loss of customers and reverse such a trend decisively.

In a nutshell, this is a situation that exemplifies what can happen when problems are not counteracted early but instead are allowed to take root and thus become monstrous.

Can Major Cost Initiatives Be Classified as Game-Changing Moves?

A game-changing move is something that confers real competitive advantage. For this reason, something that can be implemented very quickly or is trivial is unlikely to prove to be game-changing; if nothing else, your competitors will quickly copy it and you will soon be back to square one. Similar considerations apply to cost; there are industries where the cost curve improves for all competitors broadly at the same time. So, constant reduction in cost is necessary to stay viable but will not offer any advantage compared with competition. Examples of such situations include areas of high-tech industries such as semiconductors (where costs for the same performance fall on a nonstop basis) or industries where the fundamental enabling technologies are shared by many participants. You need to stay on the cost curve to remain viable, and only cost performance beyond what everybody else can achieve will offer advantage.

Now there are situations when a unique cost advantage can be established that cannot be matched by all or some of the other competitors. Examples of such situations are privileged access to raw materials or labor costs or proximity to key markets that others do not currently enjoy. Even then I have a word of caution if you make cost the centerpiece of your game-changing moves: a company that has the mindset of cost alone is not naturally geared toward innovation and creation of new markets. I believe such a company will find itself, sooner or later, outflanked by competitors in the marketplace even though these competitors may have a worse cost position at the outset.

So, getting back to the question of whether cost initiatives can be classified as game-changing moves, my answer would be twofold. First, pursue cost initiatives with gusto and make sure you have a cost basis that is better than the rest of the industry you are in. However, in most situations do not rely on cost initiatives to give you that overwhelming advantage as, most probably, they will not and others will catch up. But, you absolutely cannot prosper without establishing as low a cost position as your best competitors.

One final point on cost: although cost itself in the majority of cases is not a differentiator what you get for it (i.e., the effectiveness of the cost) can most definitely be a differentiator. This concept, of course, is what is behind the idea of free levers mentioned in Chapter 1, enhanced decision-making in Chapter 5 and the strategies suggested in Chapter 6.

Game-Changing Moves Yield Differentiation in the Marketplace

Differentiation is the key to finding game-changing moves. In many respects, differentiation is both the objective of the game-changing moves and the guiding principle for finding them. The reasons for this are simple yet profound. Ultimately, a customer will pay for the product or the service. With a plethora of choices, he or she will pay a good price only for something that excels and sets itself apart from competitive offerings.

For this reason, it is important to follow through an initiative's effect by visualizing the impact it will have in the marketplace and by asking yourself a few key questions. Will it really enable a higher level of service, quality, features or performance or offer cost advantage? Is it powerful enough to make the offering stand out (amongst many others) or, even better, is it unique enough to create a market of its own? If so, will the customer perceive these advantages, experience them and appreciate them? Or, is it something that is nice to have but does not really offer sufficient reasons for the customer to pay for it?

You also need to pay attention to which customer you are asking the questions about. It generally pays to focus on the end customer, but also take into consideration whether there are enough benefits to any others involved such as distributors, OEMs and channel partners. There must be value for all, otherwise the initiative will not succeed.

Combinations of Technology and Market Make Extraordinary Moves

Technology is a great place to locate opportunity for differentiation. When matched with the understanding of how to reach markets, how to create new markets and how to transform markets, technology becomes an extremely potent differentiation factor. In fact, it is the combination of these two forces—technology and market—that, in most industrial situations, offers the most unique and powerful results concerning differentiation.

However, for these two areas to function together, you will need for other areas, including strong operations, low cost position, customer service, the ability to market and sell effectively and a strong product-management team to come together and support the effort.

For example, in one particular point in time, my company decided we needed to wrest product leadership from our competitors. This sounds laudable but how would we achieve it?

Arithmetically, we were falling behind by introducing products on a four-year cycle while one particular competitor was doing so in 30 months. Please note that in situations where you have fallen behind, being equal will not suffice. So we knew we needed some new strategy that would result in production of a sequence of highly attractive products at a fast rate.

We quickly realized we needed a plan that looked three to five years out. We decided that instead of developing and launching a product, then starting up again, we would develop platforms that already had within them the potential to be extended and upgraded several times every eight to 12 months. The platform approach meant we would need much stronger product definition up-front, a longer development time to first product, plus greater expense to first product. But, thereafter, we would be unbeatable with fast new introductions and much lower costs.

Then we challenged ourselves. The platform approach we were proposing had been in use in other industries but (and here was a major observation) not in our industry. However, we did not want to assume we were the only guys thinking of this approach and wanted to allow for the possibility that our competitors also would switch to this very effective strategy, so we decided to go all in.

Under a complete veil of secrecy, we studied the market in depth and understood where it was and in which direction it could be moved. We then took time to carefully examine all possible technologies before choosing the path we thought would be feasible in view of technological developments. In particular, we pushed the limit in terms of product performance and cost.

We concluded that we should launch into development three platforms at once—a strategy not unlike planes lining up to land at a major airport! This approach would totally address the possible market positions. The three platforms were leading edge and pre-emptive; we skipped technology generations and pushed to the next steps. We then segmented the market and simulated how we would respond to likely moves by our competitors. If they became aggressive and went for three leading edge platforms at once— something they had never done—we would still not lose and should win some. If they were business as usual we would wrest leadership, seeing first major results in two years and completing an effective "knock out" move within three years.

To wind the story forward, in just under 24 months we delivered the first platform (totally leading edge compared with what was out there). This proved to be a major blow to our competition—an event that energized our company greatly. Competitors did not react immediately, but six months after our launch they preannounced that a product of the same technology class we had launched—essentially a "me too" product—would arrive in around 40 months from when we started and 16 months after we were in the marketplace.

But of course, by the 40-month mark, the game was essentially over. Our second platform arrived in month 32 and that served to raise the stakes yet again and put a generation of technology ahead of where our competitor would be in the 40th month. Besides, our opening launch had already captured a large part of the market.

Just as our competition was about to launch in month 40, we upped the ante yet again and launched the third platform. The game was really over for good! To quote the father of military strategy von Clausewitz, "If you want to cross a ditch do not take a half step."

To execute a strategy like the one described above, many items must come together, including the methods of development and, in this case, new production methods. Of course, you need to have in place or develop the marketing capability to effectively introduce this sort of product barrage. But it will prove worth the effort; the capabilities we developed to make this move happen carried us forward at a rapid pace for a number of years.

Technology as an Enabler Can Also Differentiate Greatly

In the previous section, I described a real-life case study exemplifying how we captured a market by introducing a product with a level of functionality beyond what was available in the marketplace. New technology enabled the product, a fact that was evident as the customer used it. However, there was another aspect of technology that enabled our long-term success. In order to produce this product, we had to invest in a new level of manufacturing technology, something our competitors missed. As a result, when our competitors came out with their products, besides being hopelessly late, the products did not achieve all the necessary performance parameters, as the level of manufacturing they employed was not as advanced as our own.

If the level of technology you use to develop or produce a product or to supply a service is ahead of that of your competitors, you own a significant advantage. Strong illustrations of this can be found in process industries where an enormous amount of technology is required for the process itself. This is also true in businesses that require a vast number of sophisticated computer systems with advanced IT capabilities.

Please note that in these examples, if a technology is shared by a large number of companies in the same industry, it is an enabler and causes companies to race to obtain it first. If the technology is unique to a certain company then it offers differentiation, but if a third party supplies the technology, the dynamics change substantially.

For instance, in some situations the underlying technology is supplied by a single vendor or a couple of vendors. Unless each individual company is capable of differentiating the technology, it too, like the cost advantage, becomes the price of being in the market rather than the reason to be excelling in the market. In fact, in some markets, you can see that a large number of companies keep introducing the newest and latest (like a camera or personal computer) but in fact there is very little difference between the products.

The performance of all products from all the manufacturers in the market rises at the same time. All the manufacturers rely on some key suppliers who really control the key technologies. The manufacturers are forced to adopt the new technologies (and in general they adopt them simultaneously) or fall behind.

If you are in a situation where the technology is shared by many of the competitors, then the game-changing activity has to concentrate on how to further differentiate it to obtain an advantage in the marketplace.

Another Way to Look at Game-Changing Moves

It is not uncommon in organizations to hear people asking questions, or making comments such as: "I am not sure we are headed in the right direction"; "Where are we going?"; "Competitor so and so is always a step ahead"; "We are permanently in catch-up mode"; "We are working hard but we are not getting the results"; "We are permanently unlucky—we took such and such initiative as the market turned", and "We believe we are not losing market share but our sales are not healthy."

These could all be signs of an organization that is in a rut and has not begun the next game-changing move, is not working toward one and may not have identified (or may not know how to initiate) the steps it needs to take to begin the process.

Traveling unarmed without game-changing moves in hand and slated to hit the marketplace within specified times, is not a secure place to be. It is a place where many setbacks will occur.

··· Chapter 8 Main Points ···

1. Game-changing moves are systematic initiatives that ensure the achievement of above market growth. Conversely, under circumstances of adverse technology and market shifts, they forestall declines.

2. Inertia is the enemy of game-changing moves. Management needs to organize its time allocation and activities to routinely prospect, identify and launch such moves.

3. It is unlikely that a single game-changing move will solve all strategic problems so a few need to be systematically identified and launched. Particular attention needs to be paid to possibilities arising from market and technology changes.

4. Game-changing moves have strong core capabilities at their foundation. It is essential to build the capabilities ahead of launching the moves. Preserving capabilities in difficult economic times also may prove to be the foundation of the future.

5. Cost initiatives, applied on their own, are unlikely to constitute a game-changing move. They are a necessary but not a sufficient condition to ensure long-term prosperity.

6. Game-changing moves can be readily identified because they offer differentiation in the marketplace.

7. A move that exploits the creation of a new market through a new technology could offer the highest level of reward.

8. It is important to look at technology in depth not only as the source of new products but also as the enabler of process.

9. If you are not consciously working on game-changing moves and executing relevant plans with specific time scales, you could be in the danger zone and very vulnerable.

· · · · ● · · · ·

In a Crisis, the Transformational Planning Toolkit Comes in Handy!

· · · · ·

I started my new position as CEO of Honeywell Specialty Materials in March 2008. This gave me a lead of six months ahead of the collapse of Lehman Brothers, an event that accelerated the decline of many of our markets.

During that six-month period, we began to look at the business differently. Under the planning framework explained in this chapter, we had taken a number of actions that already strengthened the business. This enabled us to weather the fourth quarter of 2008 relatively well, maintaining good profitability and investment rates in key areas of the business.

But in December 2008, my Electronic Materials business suffered a further setback, which occurred suddenly (almost overnight). Customer demand dropped another 40 percent, compared with 15 percent in the rest of the business. This was a major blow, and we had to address this precipitous decline very quickly.

To respond to this new challenge, we held planning sessions for about 90 minutes every other day. After each session, we committed to doing further analysis that would bolster our plan. After five such sessions, we had developed an action plan.

The action plan was solid. It identified our key assets and activities and set out to fully preserve them throughout the recession. In addition, the plan identified fundamental areas where we would have to improve to make the business more competitive.

Even as we cut expenses significantly, we kept investing in our improvement areas. Programs that supported reduced manufacturing cycle times and improved customer service received more special attention – and funding – as a result of our action plan.

While nonessential areas were put in a care and maintenance mode, business fundamentals improved dramatically. Cycle times in some of our processes were reduced from 8 weeks to 2 weeks, which gave us much more flexibility than competition.

Recessions can be jarring – no one can believe how quickly demand can drop. Equally hard to believe is how often the recovery can be equally rapid. As our business unexpectedly bounced back in the third quarter of 2009, we were able to respond much faster than our competitors, and this enabled us to gain a lot of new business from customers scrambling to find reliable suppliers.

The planning steps you need to take to get through a recession are the same as those you need in a transformation. A transformed company with strong fundamentals will not only withstand a recession better, but will also gain more strength than it would have otherwise – and more than the competition – when the economy turns around.

CHAPTER **9**

Synthesizing a Plan to Enable Transformation

Chapter Overview

Every business has a plan, although clearly some plans are more effective than others. But what is a transformational plan and how does it differ from other planning strategies? The chapter discusses what a typical plan, as generally developed by most businesses, entails. It then introduces four groups of additional activities that must be systematically defined and pursued in order to convert the normal plan into a transformational plan.

The Typical Plan

You might ask, "What is so special about the topic of plan creation that it deserves a whole chapter? Don't we all know how to plan already? What new information will be offered here?"

The purpose of this chapter is to help you establish a plan with a difference—namely, a transformational plan as opposed to a typical plan. We will begin by describing the typical plan and what it usually addresses.

Most companies generate an annual financial plan. This plan begins with a sales plan that takes into account growth in the market, new products, promotions, changes in pricing and other market initiatives. It relies on the sales pattern of the previous year and offers the best expectation available for a sales forecast. It is on the back of this plan that factories get planned, suppliers are dialed in and the overhead part of the company (i.e., items below variable cost) is determined. In addition, manpower planning is a large part of the plan. Other than raw materials (in the case of manufacturing), people costs are generally, the highest expense a business will incur.

Activities that are especially people intensive include research and development and sales and marketing. In these activities, both the number and quality of personnel have a high leverage. A typical plan provides for the key activities of the year, including customer-affinity activities, employee training, recruitment and business travel. A robust plan is one that has been thought through and is worked in detail from the bottom up. It includes capital planning and working-capital planning and it features specific inventory, receivable and payable targets.

In addition, a robust plan specifies how costs will vary from year to year and how each line on the profit and loss account will "walk" from year to year. It is specific on what is causing the cost variations year to year and is explicit as to the root causes such as additions of people, merit increases, inflation, higher levels of activity, new events or more equipment.

Even with such a thorough plan, there are major factors that must be taken into account. For one thing, the plan is highly dependent on company momentum and historic position, which, left on its own, will deteriorate. Then, too, this plan depends on the market growth rate. If this is a growth market, and the sales from year to year grow more than five to six percent, then generally under normal inflation conditions, and with reasonable cost discipline, the company will be able to produce double-digit profit growth.

As we have already discussed, a major issue exists if the natural volume growth in your market is only two percent and/or you are in a market with stronger competitors. Now you will have your hands full; you are on the receiving end of a slow market and of competition and your typical plan is not sufficient to lead you to satisfactory performance.

What do you have to do over the next few quarters to close the performance gap? Is there a way to structure or alter your plan so it can help guide you to a stronger future? The answer lies in the fact that we must discover essential elements that will turn this robust financial plan into a powerful transformational plan.

Adding Transformation Activities to the Typical Plan

Please note that most of the considerations above were centered on capturing financial numbers and building a picture of where the business will be over the planning period. The typical plan involves many activities that need to be captured, assembled, costed out and added up. It provides a framework for you to observe elements as they come together and also serves as a basis for financial control as the year progresses.

By comparison, the transformational plan brings into the fore additional variables. Some of these may be difficult to capture in the financial numbers; others will be perceived as causing an adverse financial result in the period. But, their objective is to improve substantially the position of the business during the planning period. Here is a representative list of what such a plan includes:

- Activities that lead to a new and higher level of competency in the organization

- A systematic development of new core capabilities

- A systematic closing of existing gaps

- Improvement of specific positions in the marketplace

- The funding of game-changing moves

- The institution of programs that supply constant productivity

- Disinvestment in areas with lower economic prospects

Further, a transformational plan goes on to identify specific improvements in every single area in the company. In particular, it:

- Aims to improve technological prowess, operational methodologies, costs and positions in the marketplace.

- Sponsors initiatives for repositioning the company behind game-changing moves and away from lower-return activities

The above list is not long but I believe it contains the essential, meaningful target areas that enable a better tomorrow.

After developing such a list, the next step is to review these potential activities and choose the ones that hold the most promise and offer greatest possibilities for your business. In this way, your typical plan can become an annual transformational plan. For that to actually take place, the activities you choose to include must be regarded seriously and receive full funding, and formal projects must be set up to execute.

So, how do you find the money to fund all these activities? How can you undertake all these changes when you already have enough financial commitments and are trying to meet a profit target, especially in a company in trouble?

To facilitate the selection of these programs I divide, my targeted transformational activities into four groups:

1. Identify and disinvest weak areas to improve the portfolio but also to provide funding.

2. Identify and start programs in areas that will generate annual productivity.

3. Institute programs to improve the fundamentals in the organization.

4. Invest in game-changing moves.

By definition, the four groups listed here facilitate transformation; they enable the building of capabilities, enable the continuous upgrading of the business and provide productivity and growth.

Please note that the first two activities can be regarded as sources of funding. The third may require funding, but ideally you will aim to get the improvements for free by using the free lever approach advocated in this book. The last item will definitely require funding.

Let's discuss each one of these four areas in more detail.

1. Identify and disinvest weak areas to provide funding

There are two reasons why you need to include the activity of identifying and disinvesting weak areas in your plan. Reason number one is that activities that are not economic have to be deemphasized; having a strict priority and knowing the disinvestment plan is a very healthy way to run a business.

Reason number two is the need to generate resources for higher-return activities and particularly game-changing moves. Please note that the generation of funding by this method is really a one-off event. To illustrate the point, let's say you need $2 million to invest in a new initiative. To do that, you decide to discontinue a mature activity that is just breaking even and reallocate the people and other resources. Once you make the switch, there is no more funding available from that source. Please note that if your company is in trouble, in all probability there will not be that many alternative sources of funding to these switches.

So, the switches are precious and they are pivotal: you need to obtain strong results out of the redeployment. Ideally, you need to use this money to start off the equivalent of a "chain reaction," deploying the money in ever more effective projects with higher returns. Clearly, in any such plan the first steps, and the first few activities of redeployment, are the most consequential.

2. Identify and invest in areas that will give annual productivity

As the saying goes, you can give a man a fish and he can eat for a day, or you can give him a fishing rod and he can eat forever! The activity in section 1 is the equivalent of "fish" and it provides start-up funding. It is therefore very important to identify the areas and programs that will be the equivalent of "fishing rods." Such activities generally serve to increase the expertise of the people involved on a constant basis and, through them, produce results.

For instance, the famed Toyota Production System has exactly that effect. It involves the operators in such a way that they become an integral part of manufacturing and of progress with continuous reinforcement of the lean concepts and training that bring continuous operational improvements.

There are many activities that have similar and increasingly positive long-term effects. These include continuous product improvements, systematic efforts in procurement to lower costs, product redesigns for cost and performance improvements, better IT systems, streamlined organization, etc.

A good plan chooses a number of such projects and then makes available the resources, people and milestones necessary to launch and deliver the initiatives. Fishing rods are of the essence; as you identify additional potential candidates for activities with such profile, you need to launch expeditiously.

3. Fix fundamentals

Activities that fix fundamentals begin with improving the level of decision-making in the organization. This is a major item with huge leverage. If you can continuously improve decision-making during the next few quarters, you have an annuity that only gets bigger in the years to come.

Your efforts to systematically improve the fundamentals of your organization represent a major undertaking; it is a job that, in many respects, will never reach completion. However—particularly when dealing with a broken organization—the leverage gained from concentrating on this area is large. Rather than reiterate what has already been said, I refer you to the information on enhanced decision-making (Chapter 5) and the seven strategies for producing results (Chapter 6). Implementing even a few of these strategies will result in terrific improvements in the fundamentals of your business which means you will be able to achieve a lot more with a lot less…and very soon it shows as substantial improvement in the profit and loss account.

4. Invest in game-changing moves

The next activity class involves investing in game-changing moves. These moves may not offer immediate major benefits; you may not see evidence of benefits in even one or two years. In fact, you may have to fund elements of such a move for a number of years until you realize the full benefit. In a business world that is divided into quarters, this can be a difficult task. You need to use the funding provided from improving the basics, from the areas that offer constant productivity (the "fishing rods") and from the areas of disinvestment (the "fish") to fund these moves. It can be helpful to break these game-changing moves into activities that begin to pay on the way to completion.

For instance, in an earlier position I conceived that if I put together a web of closely related distribution and manufacturing entities in Europe, in an industry that was not offering this on a transnational basis across the continent, it would offer a major competitive advantage. The advantage would come from our ability to share the back-office activities and logistics and our product lines. This would offer a broader product line than those available from our competitors, who were working on a national basis only, as well as a lower cost to procure and supply. As I began making these investments, with the network only partially completed and prior to the completion of the total project, benefits began to come through. These helped greatly with increasing profits and provided funding capability to complete the plan.

Similarly if you are repositioning your sales force, a part of that may be retraining, which on its own gives positive results even before the rest of the move is complete. Sequencing matters greatly and affects the overall cost and benefit flow of the effort.

Avoid the Pitfalls of Choice and the Need to Provide Plan "Boosters"

Opening up the planning process to the four activities mentioned in the previous section generates a lot of energy and a plethora of options. While this is exciting to see, it also requires the establishment of clear choices and firm selection of the activities that will be undertaken.

Clearly the choices you make will hinge on your organizational strengths and your market and competitive realities. Nevertheless, the choice means you start with many ideas and end with a few strong ones to implement.

A very common mode of failure, one born of enthusiasm and sometimes inexperience, is to become too exuberant and optimistic regarding what can be achieved and by when. This enthusiasm keeps adding to the tasks to the point the tasks become unmanageable, and the original objectives never get achieved.

Once you have chosen a few activities, you have to perform the affordability and risk test. These tests are interrelated because you need to have a high degree of confidence in the activities so that by the end of the prescribed time, you will realize the result you seek. It is not desirable for early transformational activities to fail, and the activities chosen must offer a high margin for error.

The first reason for this is that, particularly early on, you want your organization to go on and to win and experience success as a way to build confidence in the process. Second, success breeds success, and confidence brings more capability and more daring so the larger tasks, which might have failed at the beginning of the transformation, become securely possible.

So, if possible, your choices should avoid low-probability endeavors. Certainly, such endeavors have a place but not as the cornerstone of the transformation journey.

There is yet another reason which dictates activities have to produce results in the targeted time. This has to do with the issue of a business naturally needing financial boosters to keep going. How does this arise?

The world is full of competition, new entrants, changing markets, new products replacing old, distribution channels changing, customers moving on and shifting economic conditions. At the same time, costs may rise. If all these factors remain unchecked, they will naturally tend to drag results down, particularly in a weak company in need of transformation. The external forces are definitely against you, and no matter how strongly you believe in your plan these adverse forces will materialize sooner or later and have a negative effect on a fragile business.

A company (particularly a weak company) that does not have a planned methodology to counteract these negative forces will find itself in a weakening position. So, before the plan is finalized, I consider where it can go wrong and where it will need shoring up. In particular, I look to see where it will need some new "factor" to enter on the positive side to counteract the negative factors that are naturally thwarting our activities.

I tend to view these new positive factors as a series of time-planned boosters. I have a clear idea of when the boosters will arrive (more commonly must arrive) and their magnitude. So, these are time-sensitive projects that must give that positive result. The right mix of projects must be selected in order to deliver a booster of sufficient magnitude within the required time frame. Of course, this analysis presupposes enough of a grasp of what is going on in the company and the marketplace to be able to predict what the shortfalls are going to be.

In thinking about the future, people tend to project what has happened in the most recent few periods. If these periods were strong, then they project the strength will continue; if weak, then they project the weakness will continue. While there is some correlation between present strength and its continuation, as well as between present weakness and its continuation, actual results do not always reflect such direct correlation continuums. There is, however, a stronger correlation with respect to weakness continuing rather than strength continuing. Again, this statement is very pertinent to a fragile business.

If your business is weak or weakening you absolutely require a mix of projects, some of which are short term and will deliver results (boosters) in a couple of quarters and others which will give boosts in one, two, three or more years out.

Of the four groups of activities, game-changing moves are superlative; unfortunately they take the longest time to come to fruition as this is their nature. Ultimately, you need the mega booster that successful game-changing moves can deliver. In the interim, you may have to work very hard to keep the programs running using the other three methodologies: keep inventing programs in the areas of disinvestment and reallocation, find projects of constant productivity and improve the fundamentals.

A Practical Example

Sometime ago, I discussed this framework with a friend who has his own business in the promotional field. Over time, we have shared many discussions on how he might expand his business. He has built a strong business and, in recent years, his business has enjoyed significant growth. The business still performed satisfactorily in the downturn that started in 2007, although, like the rest of the economy, it showed signs of weakness.

The issue vexing my friend had been how to take the assets and people he has, most of them long serving, and inject new growth prospects into his business.

He is a savvy businessman who knows his marketplace very well. This gives him a great advantage compared with competition. On the other hand, he is working in a business he has grown himself with adequate but not unlimited sources of capital and personnel know-how. He was in a strong position in that he had, in principle, identified the game-changing moves to make, and wanted to proceed and establish their full potential. But, he was boxed in financially, especially in the downturn. He did not have the resources to fund new ideas; at the same time I have heard him often ask basic questions: How do I do this and how do I grow my people to be able to do more? How do I cover and service orders day to day while also prospecting for more business, all the while trying to locate resources to build for the future?

As a mature businessman he was aware that what had propelled his growth in the past may not hold in the future. He knew that his success had attracted competitors into his space and competition was catching up.

Our discussions always boiled down to two issues. He, being market savvy, knew the direction in which he wanted to take his company. This knowledge was, of course, a major advantage. On the other hand, given the organization he had in place and his financial resources, he felt limited in what he could do to improve his situation. This second piece of knowledge curtailed his enthusiasm and undermined his confidence in any new undertaking, and he knew that time was not on his side with well-funded competitors on his tail.

I discussed with him the framework suggested in this book. He was in no doubt that he needed another transformation to move his business ahead before competition caught up to him. He had to diversify and expand his sources of revenue. I laid out the four premises of the transformation plan I have expanded in this chapter.

The problem is that he needed to start somewhere and he had no funds. So, according to the premises of this chapter (turning your business into a winner by leveraging existing resources), step one is that we needed to find some areas to disinvest from. Although he was generally satisfied with the way the business ran when we looked in detail, the satisfaction in the aggregate became more granular. Some lines of business were strong and others weak. I asked him to rank the activities he was undertaking and then decide which ones to exit. Bear in mind that some of the activities he needed to jettison were profitable then, but their prospects were not strong.

This was a tough assignment both practically and emotionally. However, the knowledge that discontinuing some of these activities would provide him with the resources, in terms of people and money, to begin setting the stage for his long-term moves gave him enough motivation to continue the process.

However, the result of this analysis led to the next dilemma. As his markets develop slowly, the payback from the game-changing moves he wanted to make would take upwards of two years. This would be a long time in the wilderness for a small, private company that did not want to go to the bank or other sources of capital. So, the funding we could create by reallocation was not sufficient to fund the long-term moves he wanted to make.

Therefore, we sat down and discussed what he could do to improve the fundamentals in the business. He needed to identify activities that would increase the efficiency of what was already in place and, in the process, enable more to be achieved for less, all the while improving customer service. Again, generating a list of such projects was not easy but a credible list was produced in time. When completed, these projects would provide the prospect of a lower cost base and additional monies available on an annual basis to fund the long-term objectives.

This project list, again, could not all be afforded at once financially and, in particular, in the ability to carry them out. It required sitting back and coming up with trade-offs in activities involving better computer systems and information to run the business, more prescribed processes, clearer daily running of the business, more effective ways to run the production areas and warehousing, and stronger leadership. A final selection was made for implementation, with specific programs and resource allocation to make them happen.

The combination of implementing these activities (some basic improvements and some "fishing rods") began to show in the financial statement within 12 months. Now he had the assurance that he could undertake his game-changing moves (which will require funding for up to 24 months before they become self financing) without the fear of running out of financing and with the confidence he could see them through.

At the time of writing the plan appears to be coming to strong fruition. However, this has been very hard work of hands-on management and required the acquisition of one other key skill: the management of change. One of the reasons small and large companies are not adapting for the future (beyond recognizing the need and having the financial means to do so) is that they do not have the key management skills to initiate and guide change.

This brings us to the subject matter of the next chapter.

· · ·   **Chapter 9 Main Points**   · · ·

1. A thorough, typical business plan is a good basis for a transformational plan but it is not sufficient.

2. A transformational business plan has to enable the company to break through over time and produce growth and superior results even in stagnant markets.

3. A transformational plan includes activities that increase the competency of the organization, enhance its core capabilities and improve the standing of every key area in the company. Special attention needs to be given to technological prowess, operational methodologies, costs and the establishment of marketplace opportunities.

4. To effect transformation, it is necessary to go beyond the normal plan and target activities into four groups:

   • Identify areas for disinvestment

   • Develop areas that give constant productivity

   • Improve the fundamentals in the business

   • Invest in game-changing moves

5. A combination of the above four groups needs to be selected, as together they provide funding, increase capabilities and enable game-changing moves.

· · · · · · · ·

Changing How
an Organization Thinks

· · · · ·

It was March 2008, and I was brand new at my job as CEO of Honeywell Specialty Materials. As we've discussed throughout this book, one of my first techniques – especially when getting into a brand-new industry – is to listen carefully to the way people are talking about the business. Even casual conversations can reveal deeply held beliefs. One of those widespread beliefs within Specialty Materials at the time struck me right away as problematic. It was the belief that growth is a stand-alone enterprise.

Earlier in the decade, Specialty Materials had established a Growth Fund that cost the business $20 million annually, overseen by a Growth Board that was staffed by several members of the leadership team. The purpose was to provide seed money to people with promising growth ideas, in hopes these ideas could be incubated and grown into full-fledged businesses. A number of intelligent and well-intentioned people believed that growth ideas would be neglected if they were embedded within the businesses, and they wanted to play the role of venture capitalist, placing little bets here and there and tying additional funding to milestone achievements. The problem was, from what I could tell, there was no formal roadmap in place to define these milestones, and no underlying operating system to drive the progress of these investments. There was no philosophy that defined what made a good investment and what made a bad one. Money was dispersed, but the results – if there were any – never found their way to the income statement.

One of my first actions was to do away with the Growth Fund. Instead, I held my business leaders accountable for bringing good growth ideas forward and reallocating resources within their own businesses to drive these ideas.

We also established a phase-gate process for new product introductions that required early marketing and technology validation – including voice of the customer input – before we started investing big dollars in growth projects. We systematized this process with oversight during Business Decision Week. The idea was to make the gate reviews tough. At first, more than 50 percent of the reviews led to new projects being killed or re-directed.

Did the lack of special seed money cause our spirit of innovation to dry up? To the contrary – in 2010 alone, we rolled out more than 80 new products that collectively generated 5 percent (a large number in the Chemical Industry where product life cycles are long) of our sales even though most of these products were in the market for a small part of the year. Our new product pipeline over the next few years will generate the equivalent of 50 percent of our current revenues! At Honeywell, we believe this type of seed planting is absolutely essential to being the type of business that performs quarter after quarter after quarter.

The key to changing an organization to focus on growth doesn't revolve around Growth Funds, special campaigns or slogans. You don't need to exhort people to think differently or creatively – but you do need to give them context in which to do so. You need to make systemic changes in the way they think, the way they manage, and the way they set priorities and allocate resources.

The means by which you achieve growth is by changing everybody within the business to be a growth agent. Then growth happens throughout the organization without being a specific activity – it's everybody's business!

As we saw within Specialty Materials, the best type of change management strategy brings about change naturally, across the whole of the organization, without fuss. This chapter will dig into the details on how best to accomplish this.

CHAPTER **10**

Seven Requirements for Effective Change

Chapter Overview

So far, directly and indirectly, we have been talking about managing controlled change. Change requires a framework and this chapter identifies seven requirements for establishing a robust change framework. It covers the need for constancy of values to guide change and for establishing a strong transformational team. It sets out the requirements of how to build a confident organization and how to register the new methodologies into the DNA of the organization. In addition, it defines detailed change forums, why they are necessary and how each is used. Finally, it explains how to identify exceptional talent for change and how to instill in the organization the means to know when a change initiative has outrun its usefulness.

Preparing for Change

In the extreme, transforming a company may be described as an ongoing revolution that must be managed at every step. Particular care must be exercised at transition points such as implementing new methods, entering new markets or introducing new technologies. Some chaos can be desirable if controlled. However, it is imperative to organize the business so that it can cope with change and yet not let change go awry and cause loss of control. Change can have unforeseen and unintended consequences and these must be prevented.

The holistic changes involved in a transformation mean that a lot of people will come to work every day and channel their activities in a new manner and toward new objectives. This in turn means you need a change management framework that is comprehensive and robust. In addition, it must enable the change but also control it.

The requirements I outline in this chapter form the framework from which you can effectively advance and manage change. Being aware of these requirements and putting them in place is essential to successful implementation.

An organization that adheres to these requirements has the great advantage of being in a state of constant readiness for response to new circumstances. This readiness comes in very handy when the going gets tough, such as in times of a recession or when major unforeseen difficulties arise. In these conditions flexibility and speed of adaptation are necessary and you will have both readily available!

Requirement 1: Establish a Clear Business Philosophy in a Sea of Change

I have stated in earlier chapters that I expect in a single quarter to achieve the same progress that a normal organization makes in a whole year. I also expect that the progress will continue, quarter in and quarter out. This entails a situation of nonstop change—a situation that must be handled with care.

During a time of constant change, many intangible yet real qualities, such as morale, commitment, dedication and a sense of belonging, matter more than ever; yet, these are the qualities most threatened by the circumstances of continuous change. Too much change can disorient an organization and take it seriously backwards. In addition, if an organization does not have its heart and mind in the change, there will be push back and resistance and, as a result, progress will be slow.

So, the very real question arises of what do you do and what do you say to enable your organization to come aboard willingly and participate whole-heartedly on a long journey involving vast amounts of change? How do you handle these circumstances so you enable transformation?

The answer is that from day one, you need to clearly establish the principles along which you will run the business. This means having the principles in hand and then undertaking a systematic campaign to communicate them. The communication has to be clear and repeatable. In particular, it must have no ambiguity and be consistent from one day to the next.

You will not be surprised to hear that I begin day one by setting a brief outline of my general business philosophy. I have already explained what this philosophy is in Chapter 3 and will not repeat it here. Clearly, a business philosophy is rather a lot to explain and will take a few months before it gets fully understood; it has to be repeated many times and included in every single communication opportunity. The information is transmitted with as much brevity as possible, but I never miss an opportunity to give pertinent detail and tailor it to the audience. For instance, if I am talking to marketing people I expand on my expectations of how good marketing activity is organized and pursued.

While the philosophy is broad and covers many areas, in the first month I give a disproportionate amount of "air time" to behaviors and performance. I make sure people understand that our business will not be run on individual whims and that I want to see real economic decisions and results. I want to see new ideas and controlled entrepreneurship. I want to see strong decisions made with real facts. I want to see speed and imagination, yet no errors. I want to see a culture of achievement. But, with all the above, I make sure people understand that their future and promotions will be based on objective grounds and results and not on personal whims. Secondly, I give "air time" to the key operating processes I will introduce (particularly Business Decision Week, discussed in Chapter 4) and how this will help all of us to move forward.

My message is one of confidence and encouragement. Confidence that there is a much better future and encouragement that as we collectively work together to make it happen, there will be benefits for the organization. I reinforce my message daily and, like a mosaic, the detail gets filled in with every single action and meeting. This is about repeatability and consistency.

All the above parts of my message unfold over a number of months and become reinforced day in and day out thereafter. The effect is that the organization understands what the ground rules are and it stands "on a solid platform" from which to navigate a sea of change. Everyone knows what the new game is and what its regulations are. People also know that if they join the game and play well, they will participate in the upside.

I have one final point that is especially relevant if you are entering a new organization: establish the ground rules of how you will handle extant personnel. The conventional wisdom is that a new leader will introduce new management; this expectation can destabilize an organization and make it ineffective. My approach on the matter is very simple: I walk into a new position with the genuine intent of keeping the existing team provided they can act as transformational leaders, and I explain what that involves. I change team members reluctantly and only after establishing they cannot meet the required standards.

Requirement 2: Establish a Management Team of Change Agents

The amount of change that can be driven in an organization depends on management attitudes, orientation and expertise. All of these attributes can be influenced and improved; managers who do not have experience in change management can become change agents. On the other hand, not everybody is suited to the role.

The framework for selecting strong change agents is subtle but crucial. What is the framework and how do you make this determination? Let's imagine you have arrived fresh into a new position and are trying to establish a team to lead a transformational journey. You need to ascertain if the incumbents are capable to assist you today, or whether they may become so tomorrow. As I explained previously, in the first requirement, the first item is to establish some firm principles. The interpretation of these principles is, in and of itself, the beginning of a test. Principles are always subject to interpretation; the ability to correctly interpret these principles in situations of ambiguity (a manifestation of judgment) is one criterion of suitability for managers in key leadership positions.

The shared understanding is that the principles have been chosen to guide us but that they do not revolve around my senior team or me. They are there to improve the business and the way we all function and manage within the business. The business is neither a dictatorship nor a democracy but an organization that listens to all ideas, selects the best (fast!) and executes to plan.

I stress that financial results are the consequence of taking the correct actions to win markets and to service customers effectively, so we have to concentrate on how to do these things and do them well. Also, I am particularly sensitive as to whether or not the senior management team is capable of understanding backstops and risks, which I explain below as Requirement 7 as this is another area that requires strong judgment.

The above are not negotiable and members of my management team have to be able to operate within these principles.

In parallel, I also undertake a program to systematically challenge the team. It has often been said that visualization of the future and prediction are the basis of intelligence. Without conceiving of a better future and developing options of how to get there, you will never transform a company. It is for these reasons that the area I like to probe most is that of forward thinking.

Forward thinking is more rarely found than appears at first glance, but it is a gift that many possess naturally. It is a core competence, not only of successful business people, but also of the great leaders in history. These visionaries could simply see where tomorrow would go and how to position themselves to benefit from it. After I provide my executives with examples of forward thinking in action, I ask them to take their plans and devise three key strategies within their area of responsibility that would position us better in the future. The challenge is laid out with scenarios that assume financial constraints and no financial constraints.

This task becomes a litmus test to find out if people have the imagination to visualize the future and show they can take the necessary steps to position the business better. I have performed this exercise many times. Here are a handful of typical reactions:

- Some managers become very defensive and start justifying why they made certain decisions in the past and why these decisions were correct when, in essence, the outcome was not.

- I have had managers claim that what they had been doing is perfect. The implication is, how dare I, who just arrived at the company (and by implication a clueless person) question that?

- I have had other managers who simply had difficulty grasping the question, its implications and how to handle it (clearly, this is a very inauspicious start).

- I have had managers say this approach was very interesting and liberating. They seriously set themselves to work to find out the best ways to respond.

- Strong managers are usually there already. Before you have time to finish, they set out what they would like to achieve and why, and what they need to do it.

- Instead of addressing the issue, some managers spent the time trying to work out the reason behind this approach and what would be the political and turf implications.

- There is finally the classic response, especially in organizations that have been run top down: people try to guess what you want to hear and come up with something to fit the guess. They spend endless hours in a divination game and substance is ignored.

This simple test is a great, early indicator of the change of attitude and orientation that needs to take place by a few members of the team. This is certainly a situation where I mark the calendar. I will exercise every opportunity (through one-on-one discussions, by working in tandem on particular tasks and through choice of objectives) to put people in the right frame of mind to become effective transformation agents. It will come down to their capability to manage new concepts, attitude, mental agility, orientation and fortitude to lead substantial change. But, they need to come aboard with the change program in reasonable time and achieve the level of required attitude and orientation. I normally allow a 5- to 9-month window.

However, as I said before, not everyone can make the required changes nor does everyone possess the capability to act as a change agent. Personnel changes may have to be made despite the loss of long-term knowledge and the risk of possible organizational upheaval.

Requirement 3: Build a Confident Organization

The first step in building a confident organization starts with developing confidence in the leadership.

For the leader, this means winning the confidence of people around him or her and doing so quickly. Ultimately, confidence is won by people realizing the leader knows exactly what he or she is doing and sees the way forward for the long term. People up and down an organization get very excited the minute they see results, the capabilities of the organization increase, or the correct decisions being made.

It is a very heartening experience when the executive team begins to get the idea of how the whole transformation process works and they see the first glimpses of real success. They may not yet see the whole journey but, as belief and confidence build, the results accelerate.

I always know that we are on a great winning path (way before the results show) because competent people jump onboard of their own free will; they realize this is something that will help the company and that they will learn a lot in the process. They tell me that this experience is an asset they can use now and in the future as they further their personal careers. Before I know it, the enthusiasm moves to the next level and teams are vying for excellence and for a spot to present both to the executive team and during BDW. Then I know I have momentum.

As momentum gathers it is time to capitalize on it. However, in the early days momentum is fragile and can reverse easily. To maintain it, there is a need to foster the right behaviors and support the organization's increasing confidence. Just as success generates success, confidence generates confidence. The two go together. So, how do you ensure that they both take place simultaneously?

If any of us look back on our early days in the classroom, we would observe that our learning took place by steps and in increments. An eighth grader will normally get very frustrated and feel like a failure while doing an 11th grade level assignment. Giving people who are set in their ways (and who probably never had sufficient tools in place to begin with) projects they are not yet capable of handling is exactly how managers unwittingly destroy confidence. It does not mean these people will never be capable of handling these projects; it just means that now is not the right time.

Ultimately, it really does not matter what grade you start from. What matters is how fast you progress through the grades and whether you are outpacing competitors by a large factor.

Now, an organization does not zoom through the grades just because a manager says so! It requires some activities to achieve this. Learning by doing is a great means to increase knowledge and bring tangible results to the bottom line. An organization does not learn or progress fast by bringing in third parties to do its work; change happens at a much faster pace by undertaking developmental projects with ideas and execution generated primarily from within.

So, it all comes down to choosing and pursuing a series of projects (in practice, a few key projects at a time) that are meaningful to the future of the business. You need to set up teams and challenge members with the responsibility to execute achievable projects. This approach is particularly important while organizational confidence is still building.

In defining and running these projects, it is important to provide formal support at regular intervals. It is the occasion to make constructive comments and set expectations. In particular, it is the time to iron out the issues of common terms and well-defined communications. It is the time to begin aligning processes and activities. All these items appear small and simple, but they cannot be bypassed as they are foundational. In addition, with these activities you are bolstering the spirit of confidence and of achievement on which success is built.

One final comment on confidence: do not unleash your ego in the face of budding confidence. It is remarkable how frequently I have come across managers who were masters at destroying confidence and thus condemning themselves to failure. Destruction of confidence is easy to do, particularly by people with big egos who want to prove they are never wrong. When things go well, they claim it is because of them, and when they go badly, everybody else is to blame. These and similar behaviors do not nourish confidence or encourage achievement in an organization. Work to keep your ego in check.

Requirement 4: Build Cohesive Culture and Trust

In a transformation, you clearly want to change the culture and make it a daily contributor to improvements. I set out on the culture I aim to establish in Chapter 1 and here it is again: "They know what they are doing, they are task orientated, they work effectively in teams and they address problems succinctly and will not use two hours where one will do. In addition, they look forward; they think of alternatives; they examine opportunities; they are agile, systematized, and organized and they pay close attention to their decision-making process. Interpersonally, they are demanding of each other but respectful and appreciative of the individual; they know when to take risks and they are proud to be part of a team that grasps opportunities."

Whether you want the type of culture I am looking to establish or something different, the question that arises is how do you modify culture to what you want and how do you make it robust so that it does not revert?

All the actions, processes and methodologies suggested in this book will contribute to the establishment of a new culture. I do, however, have a simple observation that has led me to be especially aware of when it is a good time to affect culture: people always remember difficult times; they particularly remember how others behaved–especially towards them.

As the saying goes, a friend in need is a friend indeed! When the times are good it is easy for everybody to be great. The real test comes when the times are hard. In particular, how does an organization react when there are difficulties in meeting objectives and setbacks occur? I have seen bosses who simply "lose it" under difficult circumstances, becoming divisive. This is one of the worst behaviors you can have because it destroys any possibility of future credibility and trust. An organization with leaders behaving this way will never be successful.

A time of setbacks is by far the best time to build an esprit de corps and the culture of the business. It is really the time when those indelible memories are formed. How did my boss and my colleagues behave toward me when my area of responsibility ran into trouble? Did they offer to help (genuine help!) or were they running away and throwing stones on their way? Events like these do happen and really remove any possibility of trust and cooperation and, disable the change potential.

When there is an acute problem, it is not the time to finger point. It is the time to get the best expertise possible around the table to address it selflessly. It is amazing how much leverage you get from an organization that knows that when it experiences a problem (whether as a consequence of its own actions or external factors), the wagons will be circled and the best know-how will be applied to address it. This is not a time to backstab anybody, apportion blame or make accusations; rather it is a time to simply address the issues at hand effectively.

Trust builds greatly in these circumstances. Trust also enables huge progress all the time, even when there are no immediate problems.

Please note that a practice of being trigger happy and firing people routinely when they run into trouble has another negative effect: under those conditions, management will hide the trouble for as long as it can. This only serves to make the solution much harder to reach. The key to trouble resolution is to perceive the problem early and immediately put in place the appropriate countermeasures.

I aim to build an organization that has the trust to use all its resources to move fast, fight out of a tight spot and win. This culture can be built most effectively in difficult times and then, once you establish it, it becomes a very powerful weapon. If there is one predictable thing in business it is that there will be setbacks. A team that routinely knows how to put adversity behind it so to address these setbacks with verve, gusto and speed is a winning team. I want to be on that team!

One final point in favor of this approach: when there are acute difficulties and the team pulls together to find the solution, normally you acquire knowledge that stays with an organization forever. The learning is memorable and serves as the way to tackle similar situations in the future. This is yet another benefit to come out of crisis.

Requirement 5: Establish and Use Change Methodologies

This section addresses the methodologies used to effect change. The methods I advocate fundamentally rely on two pillars. First, use the leader (and eventually the broader leadership team) as a coach. Second, turn the culture of the organization into one of continuous learning.

However, to be able to implement these methodologies, you must have a clear idea about how an organization learns. Although there is room for all established means of learning (lectures, courses, projects, case studies, etc.), I prefer the ones that involve interactive learning by doing as the primary means. It is for this reason that I have split this section into four subsections, placing most of the emphasis on the first two of the four methodologies as outlined below.

Methodology 1: Change through the operating mechanism

If you decide to set up the BDW method as your operating mechanism, as advocated in Chapter 4, then you have established the most effective method for change management possible! Certainly, it would be a shame not to use these 10 weeks in the year (which, after all, is a considerable amount of time, far exceeding any that would be available for external courses or other means of change) as your principle means of change management.

I do not want to repeat here the main benefits of the BDW system explained in Chapter 4, but I want to highlight a few points to raise the awareness of change management possibilities during it.

First, the agenda is topical and relevant and aims to address all the key, current and future needs of the business. This is not an outside course based on somebody else's case study. Every single project and discussion during the week is a live case study with live, directly affected participants. The subject matter is 100% pertinent to the business and so are the discussions and conclusions.

Second, in successive meetings, the same and similar issues can be looked at from different practical situations; robust conclusions and learning can be established and ingrained in the organization. This raises the competence of the participants who then take advantage of other situations available in other parts of the organization or in future opportunities they perceive.

Third, the frequency of BDW should be very high so the learning does not get forgotten between meetings. That way, much like in a fast moving class, you can move the subject matter to new topics and build an ever broader know-how. This establishes new methods without fear that the participants will forget the basics.

Fourth, there is the equivalent of examination for just about everything during BDW because very similar "live" situations will appear again and again and the organization will show if it can tackle them with more ease the next time around. When this happens, it is a signal to move the agenda on to new topics and yet new learning.

Now match that with any other change method!

Methodology 2: Change through institution of new processes

The visibility afforded through BDW soon shows where a company is lacking in the ways it handles key elements of its business. This may have to do with how it handles new investments, product launches, product development, loading factories, receivables, inventories, market research, sales, etc. How does this become so obvious? Well it is not rocket science.

If you organize presentations from, say, three groups on a similar situation (e.g., the launch activities for a new product or the way you develop products) and if you have not established optimal processes and practice, it soon becomes painfully apparent. If there has not been sharing of best practice, it is again apparent. If people have the need for guidance and are unsure, again, it will show.

This is the time to get a multifunctional team together to establish what needs to be done. This endeavor may take a few months to define, a few months to develop and then a few more months, if not longer, to establish in the organization. One key essential is the involvement of senior management. Another is if these processes are pivotal, you want their progress and introduction monitored through BDW.

It is incredible to me how much lift you get in execution and how much risk reduction you experience when you have a few well-defined and thought-out approaches to the key activities involved in running your business. These new processes have to be firm in nature but, as always, allow for judgment and common sense to prevail over a mechanistic approach.

Clearly, introducing new processes entails large amounts of change for the organization. To the extent that managers are involved in the design of what they will implement, you are that much better off in the implementation. Again, a word of warning is in order: choose your battles as you cannot go around changing everything at once; a few (but no more than three) well-chosen activities at a time (which may take a few quarters) will yield results.

Methodology 3: Change through internal courses

I am not a great fan of classroom learning. I like learning by doing, and the way I run a business has often been likened to a continuous business-school project. Projects and processes we address become cases that are constantly "showcased" in the organization through the operating mechanism; we have no end of real, live cases and they provide great learning while addressing the needs of the business. These cases help us break into new ground to establish new ways of doing things. There is benefit all around.

I reserve classroom courses for special situations when we have a succinct message to offer to many people as we bring them up to speed with new ideas. What we teach is generally internally developed and specific to those areas where we want to accomplish change; we provide a class forum where we introduce the new ideas to a lot of people at once. This learning has to be followed by constant usage and adoption in our daily routines. If it is not, the retention is very low and it becomes another course people went to and, in a matter of weeks, forgot about.

The preceding comments may sound negative but they are not. Use this methodology when you are sure exactly what it is you want to achieve and know exactly how you will adopt and reinforce it after people leave the classroom setting.

Methodology 4: Change using outside agents

For all of the above, there are situations where an organization cannot initiate the change from within. It simply does not even understand that its DNA is missing some key links. When you do not know, you simply do not know and are not even aware you do not know, let alone have the knowledge to initiate change.

As a leader, you may have a sense that something serious is amiss and that a key core capability is not there. You might even know roughly what is missing, but being able to fix it is another matter. Further, you cannot find anybody internally who possesses the experience to lead the organization into the required changes.

This is when you have to go outside. My first advice is to take a lot of time finding the right solution and to talk to as many people as practicable. If you can identify a leader who is an expert in the field, and then attract him, it may offer the solution you need. You need someone with deep know-how, credibility and management skills. The right person might be able to arrive and gain traction pretty fast.

One question I often get is whether a person like this should be in an advisory (consulting) capacity or a line capacity. If the area requires long-term work and day-to-day management to achieve the changes, then my vote is always to go for an internal position. There is no doubt that an internal person will have clearer accountability and the authority to act. It is also in tune with the philosophy of change through the existing management, as they are responsible for the transformation activities.

A consulting firm may be very helpful with specific changes where there is no internal know-how or when the activities to be performed are simply too specialized. Again, selection of the right consultants is paramount. The key issue beyond the intrinsic ability to do the work is whether you are getting a product that is usable more than once. Ideally, you would like to obtain the required know-how for future use. Again, to use the analogy of the previous chapter, you do not want a fish but a fishing rod.

Requirement 6: Identify and Promote Transformational Players

I know there are many different ways to select transformational people and everybody has his or her own approach. I want to share here the qualities I look for in identifying transformational managers. Bear in mind, you do not need very many managers with strong transformational skills to radically change a very large organization. But, you need to place the ones you have in high leverage positions so they can make change happen.

One of the key reasons to be cognizant of these qualities, besides identification, is the fact that such players can be misunderstood. If I hear that somebody is difficult to manage, I immediately want to find out more about him or her. Generally, people who feel the need for change become uneasy and difficult in staid situations (not that this formula works all the time as sometimes the individual is simply difficult).

The following list of attributes I have is extensive and may be next to impossible to find in a single individual. If you do run across individuals with most of these attributes (and in my experience this is an event that occurs once or twice a year), it makes sense to hire them into the organization immediately. If you do not have a position open, you would be wise to create one for this sort of person.

The attribute list has been refined over a number of years and has been tested over a few more. In other words, it works. I have split the list into four sections. Within each section, the attributes mentioned may overlap, but essentially they are each addressing a different dimension.

The first section deals with visualization and analytics, the second with people and leadership, the third with domain knowledge and the fourth with strictly personal qualities.

Visualization and analytics

A) Ability to work from first principles

I find that a lot of people have been trained to work a certain way and do not regularly question the fundamental reasons why a specific approach has been taken. Leadership that regularly reexamines reasons and questions (in a controlled fashion) all methods followed can make huge progress. There is a class of people who readily reduce anything they see to first principles and try from there to see new implications. These are generally the people who will see new possibilities first and are those who look and really see. They are the ones who go to the heart of a situation very quickly and do not get distracted by spurious facts. They can do that because they understand the basics.

B) Agility in thinking (speed of thought and of adoption of new ideas)

This is the ability to look at different situations, some familiar and some unfamiliar, and connect with what is happening. Because these individuals understand the fundamentals, they work quickly to synthesize what is involved. Although someone may not have worked in a market or have intimate knowledge of a technology, he or she quickly asks a few questions and triangulates from the known to the unknown and, in that way, gains a firm understanding. This quality is exemplified by strong synthesis skills. The person involved quickly puts together a number of scenarios and calibrates the ranges and possibilities. What may take one person days to accomplish (while still reaching the wrong conclusion), someone with the gift of agility can correctly accomplish it in seconds.

C) Ability to see big and small and know what is what

It is surprising to me how some people confuse matters that are consequential with those that are not. A transformational person will absolutely need to differentiate daily between what is major and what is not, and act accordingly. A large part of a transformational journey is exactly the ability to concentrate on making the material items happen while not spending energy on the rest.

D) Constancy of view

People who constantly change their position (even when presented with the same set of facts) are not suited for the job of transformational leadership. Transformation happens over a long period of time, but it happens precisely because you have the conviction (and the confidence in your conclusions) to step down the same path daily. It also means that the analysis and conclusions are based on solid grounds and understanding rather than on fads.

E) Street smarts and practicality

It requires knowledge and sophistication to solve a lot of problems. However, it often requires something beyond intelligence; this something is street smarts and the ability to make things happen in a practical way. This quality manifests itself as an ability to circumvent obstacles. There are people who are very good at doing this.

F) Common sense

Above everything else, there is the requirement of common sense. Common sense is called common, but it is anything but. Common sense is not about intelligence. How do you identify people having or lacking this dimension? The best example I can give is of people who recognize what they see, who know when something is too good to be true, and who reconsider before they take action.

People and leadership

A) People skills

Transformation is about managing people and transporting them to a new destination. It is about instilling new ideas—an esprit de corps of excellence—and it is about increasing the competence of the organization and making it effective. This is a classic change-management situation. Some people can do this naturally and are able to handle these situations effortlessly; they also do it in a way that others find genuine and inspiring. This is exactly the person you need.

B) Inclusive but decisive

There is no way that anybody will be able to effect a long-term change that survives without involving the people affected and being inclusive in the decisions taken. On the other hand, there needs to be an edge and timely and decisive action. This is a balance that some people are able to reach and others are not. Strong leadership often arises because these dimensions are balanced well.

C) Taking the complex and making it simple

Communication is a key item in being able to transform. It is about explaining to others what you want done and putting it in a way that they understand and can do something with. I have often seen management personnel who unwittingly (or sometimes on purpose to impress) obfuscate or are unable to distill the essence; people cannot learn from or obtain clarity of direction from that brand of management.

Domain knowledge

A) Strong knowledge of the domain

If you are looking for transformational players in marketing or technology, it is almost always essential that they have strong knowledge of their subject. I know there are situations where people without knowledge in a field can do very well, the reason they succeed is that they bring with them an overwhelming strength in the other attributes listed in this section. In particular, they have extraordinary agility of mind and exceptional ability to see the fundamentals. In general, however, strong domain knowledge enables a lot, speeds up decision-making and avoids errors.

B) Knowledge adjacent to the domain

This is a subtle but necessary attribute. A person who is an expert in a field will not make a transformational manager without a strong understanding of how his or her actions affect adjacent fields. The reason for this is very simple: people need to have empathy and knowledge to enable them to work with the departments around them to get the optimal results. For instance, a strong sales manager needs to have understanding of how the supply chain works to be able to optimize his or her efforts. In the technical fields, the bonds with adjacencies have to be even closer. For instance, it is not sufficient to have a strong design leader for new products; to be effective, a leader needs to know the processes of putting them into production.

Personal qualities

A) High levels of energy

It goes without saying that a person attempting to transform a company is a person on a mission. I have mentioned a number of times the idea that everything is time related. There is a requirement for urgency and focus. Despite having setbacks along the way, the objectives have to be met on time and this requires dedication and a high level of energy to effect.

B) Ability to take setbacks

I always feel better when I recruit staff members who have had setbacks and have demonstrated that they can take the setbacks, make something of them and come out even better than before. Such incidents are not only demonstrations of flexibility and adjustment but also of the courage to lead out of a tight spot. In general, the ability to take setbacks dovetails with self-confidence. But, the ability to manage setbacks represents a resiliency that goes beyond mere self-confidence!

I know this is a rather long list but people possessing the majority of these attributes, although rare, do exist. They make a huge difference. Grab them!

Requirement 7: Establish the Backstops to Change

Where does change begin and where does it end? When do you or anyone else in the organization know when to stop it? When does the quest for efficiency, profit, markets and everything else a business strives for come to an end, or rather, should it come to an end?

It is not uncommon to see organizations that have driven change too far. In these instances, what started as a well-thought-out initiative becomes a tyrannical way of running a business. As a result, value is destroyed and the business becomes uneconomic. Let me discuss a couple of examples I have come across.

I have seen situations in which executives do not know when and how to stop in areas such as spending of capital. They have some assets and sometime in the past the CEO gave his business some directives on capital-spending ratios (such as new capital compared with depreciation). At the beginning, these ratios worked well and achieved the objective of improving economics. But then the ratio game took on a life of its own. People stopped looking at the fundamental economics and spent their time on how to improve the ratio.

This is an example of an initiative that eventually destroyed value as the business became disconnected from reality. Although the ratios still looked good, the business had become uncompetitive. Managers still worked hard to send the right ratios to their bosses, and the latter were in a fool's paradise thinking they knew how to run a business.

What went wrong in this example is something that is repeated daily thousands of times in businesses everywhere: the bosses did not think of putting in place a backstop mechanism. In every major initiative there must be the methodology of how to stop it so it is not able to acquire an uneconomic life of its own.

If that example, common to industrial companies, does not sound familiar, then there are other examples that have been more visible. A number of the Wall Street firms that went bankrupt took the conscious decision a few years earlier to make strategic moves into new areas and leveraged to unsustainable levels. When you begin an initiative like this, the question that arises is what are the mechanisms that need to be put in place to moderate and control such initiatives? Clearly, not enough of this type of thinking was instituted in a number of those institutions. In a couple of isolated cases, though, the circuit breakers went off and action was taken in time to get off the juggernaut; the risk was recognized and mitigated.

The ultimate backstops to change—and what must regulate in-depth change in a company—are ingrained beliefs and knowledge with respect to the law, ethics, economic sustainability, appreciation for business risk, well understood company philosophy (particularly towards open communications) and the development of judgment. Now this is a long list, but I want to draw attention to the last two.

Judgment is the glue that binds good decision-making with successful control of change for the long term. It is a license an organization needs to earn in order to become empowered and effective. Judgment will not develop if the managers do not have ingrained in their DNA the right and the obligation to push back if any instructions, decisions or initiatives violate laws, violate ethical standards or are not economically sustainable in the long term or entail undue business risks. This is why it is fundamental to have an organization that operates with openness because, without such openness, the organization will stumble seriously sooner or later.

··· Chapter 10 Main Points ···

1. A transformation journey entails constant change. This can happen only if employees participate and know where they stand. It is important to set out and establish the values and principles that will guide and survive the change. These are the constant factors in a sea of change. A strong business philosophy normally forms the backbone of these values and principles.

2. Effective change requires a management team of change agents. Identify the members of the team who are capable of becoming change agents. In principle, it is more desirable to keep the same team and change the way they operate than to replace team members. Nevertheless, team members who cannot act as transformation agents have to be replaced.

3. A confident organization will adopt and propagate change. To build confidence, it is paramount to ask the organization to accomplish continuously harder, stretching projects but which are within its reach.

4. A crisis is a key time to build DNA and trust. Behavior during a crisis should reinforce the desired values. This includes early recognition of problems without retribution and the selfless bringing to the table of the foremost expertise to tackle them.

5. Besides using the executive team as change agents and coaches, the chapter advocates another four methodologies to effect change, with emphasis on the first two:

- Use the operating mechanism (BDW) to define and monitor meaningful projects, to learn by doing and to spread knowledge widely in the organization.

- Select and establish processes for the key functions in the business with deep involvement of the people affected.

- Change through internal courses while keeping in mind that classroom learning needs to be heavily reinforced in the field to solidify impact.

- Use outside agents when the organization does not possess the internal expertise.

6. It is paramount to identify transformational managers and place them in high-leverage positions. The chapter identifies the key qualities ideally possessed by an effective transformational manager.

7. Change must be pursued with inbuilt backstops so the organization knows how far to go. Ultimate backstops include respect for the law and ethics, appreciation for economic sustainability and risk, company philosophy and, in particular, the development of judgment.

· · · ● ● ● · · ·

CHAPTER 11 IN CONTEXT
A Wake-Up Call Enhances Global Competitiveness

· · · · ·

It was December 2005. I organized a series of one-on-one meetings with the presidents of major U.S. companies to thank them for their business. I visited one particular customer that we had a close collaboration with. I spent quality time with the president of this large business, and we discussed future plans and how we could work together to develop some new air conditioning systems and controls. After the meeting concluded, I was very satisfied with the strength of our relationship and the prospects for solid cooperation in the future.

A few weeks later, I found myself traveling in the Pearl River Delta in Southern China. I had recently completed an acquisition of a company in the region, and I decided to visit another company that serviced our markets. When we arrived at the facility, the owner was pleased to see us. Within a few minutes, he proposed that we stop manufacturing a number of products and start sourcing from him instead because he could offer great prices.

We toured his facility and quickly saw that his business was based on reverse engineering Western products – mostly Honeywell's products – and then selling them for less. I was not impressed by the breadth of what he was producing, but he clearly had appeal in the marketplace, particularly in China. Like every Chinese business he had great ambitions to capture export customers.

As we were about to leave, I looked in his office and noticed our latest products in fresh Honeywell packaging. "How did you get those products?" I asked.

Our host replied with a great smile that the company I had visited in the United States a few weeks earlier had sent them. "They sent them to me so I could copy them, and then they will give me all your business," he proclaimed.

His words stayed with us as we piled into the van for the long drive back to the airport. My colleagues were seething. Needless to say, I was not ecstatic, but I was thankful that we ran across this situation. I wondered about the extent to which this situation was repeating itself each day. Clearly, the domestic market in China had grown to the point of being able to support domestic manufacturing for this type of product. It was time for action.

One option was to start procuring from this supplier and resell the product, but we did not do that. Another option was to conclude that everything made in China would be cheaper and therefore would prevail and shut our North American and European factories, but we did not do that either. Instead, we decided that it was time to add a factory in China to service the Chinese market. Within 18 months, we were on stream, and our Chinese engineering center worked very effectively to produce great new products suited to that market.

The new Chinese factory boosted our global offerings, enabling us to provide service on every continent. This was something our customers valued—a lot. Remember the U.S. company that I visited—the ones who sent our products to our Chinese competitor in hopes they could get cheaper reverse-engineered alternatives? They had a bad experience with our competitor and ultimately came back to Honeywell. I wasn't surprised. We had responded in an effective way to sustain our global competitiveness.

CHAPTER **11**

Sustainability and Continuous Transformation

Chapter Overview

A transformation is never totally complete; in some industries the competitive dynamics are such that a fast pace of change has to be maintained permanently while, in others, a position of strong leadership may afford a less intensive pace of change. This chapter sets out five steps to ensure sustainability, including monitoring the environment and the crucial step of recognizing structural shifts. It ends with suggestions on how to maintain competitiveness in structural shift situations.

When Does a Transformation Become Complete?

In Greek mythology, Sisyphus was a man who could never win. He was required by the gods to push a huge boulder up a hill. To obtain liberation, he had to install the boulder at the top. However, before he reached the top, the boulder would slide back down to the bottom. He would then turn around and start over again and again. In other words, for all eternity, he was condemned to never obtain his goal.

Is this a good framework for a transformation journey? Are the forces of competition the modern gods? Competitive forces now emanate from all the corners of the globe and demand that the journey never really ends. Fortunately, however, the severity of the effort can afford to ease under certain circumstances and it can achieve levels of sustainability.

In fact, if you are feeling like Sisyphus, your transformation journey has not got you too far. You have made minimal progress. On the other hand, if you are feeling that you have reached the top of the mountain but your competitors have not, then you have achieved substantial progress in the journey. If you have already dedicated yourself to carrying the boulder onto a new, higher mountain, while your competitors are rolling back down the first one, then you have really achieved something of substance!

A transformation is never complete, but if you have developed an organization that has learned to push the boulder up the hill at a superior rate to the competition, and if you are able to constantly discover higher mountains to tackle (effortlessly!), then I would say a transformation has been achieved.

Are All Transformation Efforts the Same?

It is not only that some boulders are heavier than others; the hills can be steeper, too. In other words, the forces of competition in certain industries and industrial structures can be very tough taskmasters.

A transformation effort can go into the sustainability phase only when you have established sufficient distance between your company and your competitors. The difficulty of the task you have to accomplish to achieve a transformation will generally also be a strong predictor of the level of the sustainability task. The two are related, as they have to do with the level of your industry's competitiveness as well as its dynamics.

Unfortunately, some industries are condemned to very intense, competitive dynamics and, even if you are considerably ahead of your competitors, you will never achieve a level of comfort. For instance, an industry such as consumer electronics has all the characteristics of intense competition. It is a "treadmill" industry. The minute you stop running you will be overrun. Additionally, you need to reach the top of the mountain by a specific time (and certainly no later than your competitors) or you will likely fall a long way behind. If your competitors get there first and set course for the next peak before you even get to the first, your climb becomes very arduous and may threaten your viability.

For instance, the open distribution model of consumer electronics does not offer a haven if you fall behind. Your product will simply be thrown off the shelf and superior products will take its place. Given that there is a limited number of major retailers (in most developed markets) and they are constantly looking for new products to give them an edge, they will not hesitate to switch the shelf space to a hot, new product. The consumer will also run to the newest offerings. Needless to say, to the victor go the spoils and the loser has nowhere to go.

In this sort of business, transformation is about learning to run faster than competition; sustainability is about running at full speed (which also means effortlessly, as otherwise it would not be sustainable). You also must run forever at full pace.

There are many other situations where you have many more opportunities to put distance between you and your competitors. These are circumstances where errors can be forgiven and one or two errors (like falling behind in product technology) will not immediately prove mortal. The structure of the industry will afford you some time to get your act together so you can start running to catch up. This implies you need to do enough to run faster than competition during catch-up phases.

Examples of forgiving situations would include those in which a customer invests a great deal of time and money into the product, such as in the case of computer software. Even if a better alternative becomes available, the cost to change is huge and the deficiency of the system in use has to be major to justify a change. Similarly, in situations where a whole system of distribution and support need to be trained to deliver a product or a service, the cost of change will afford room for not being the best for a short while. There are of course other situations in which such barriers to entry (or exit) are huge. And yet, as we have seen in the case of the motor industry, even a huge lead like the one enjoyed by some American manufacturers was chipped away year in and year out until whole enterprises collapsed.

5 Steps to Ensure Sustainability

I regard the objective of a transformation to be the establishment of a profitable business with strong growth momentum ahead of its competitors in capabilities and prospects. If you are fortunate enough to be leading such a company, or even better, if you have transformed a company that has now reached this status, how do you maintain the lead? What I provide below is a kind of checklist to be used after the objective of the transformation has been achieved.

1. Establish Market Metrics: Share, Customer Preference and Satisfaction, Quality

The most common areas to keep a continuous eye on are the areas of market share, customer preference and satisfaction, and quality of product compared to competition. These metrics are a requirement, although it may not be possible to establish them accurately in some industries.

My observation about these metrics is that they are generally used wisely, but sometimes companies either ignore what the metrics say or extrapolate too much information from them.

Ignoring comes when, after a period of success, the metrics start to turn negative and they are perceived as a temporary phenomenon that will correct itself. This is particularly true in the area of quality, where unfavorable quality comparisons can be ignored, as, in the short term, the customer may not have the ability or willingness to switch.

On the other hand, extrapolating too much information from market metrics can be equally dangerous. In many situations, such as in the consumer electronics business I cited previously, the fact that you have lost market share is information that may have arrived too late. It is past-looking information and you should have already known that you needed to make a technology or market transition to maintain share. Today's market share is no indication of tomorrow's success and if you wait for the figures to come out, the result could be catastrophic. It is for this reason that I believe that it is a more robust approach to establish a thorough understanding of business cycle and industry cadence.

2. Understand the Business Cycle and Industry Cadence

In most industries, the introduction of new products has a cadence. It is generally dictated by the economics of the industry and the competence of the participants. It is very instructive to understand the range of possibilities. To go back to the hapless auto industry, some of the competitors were introducing new products every three to four years and others every six to eight. Now, you do not need to wait for market share indicators to find out which one is going to win over 15 to 20 years. You know in advance that the three- to four-year company will win. In addition, you can most definitely predict the market share trend way before some external agency reports it 15 years later.

A transformed company has leading metrics in terms of cadence; it has the shortest cycles and is the leader by constantly introducing innovations. To keep winning it needs to stay there and continue improving at a pace that is at least comparable to that of competition. Of course, this implies that the disciplines developed during the transformation phase are well ingrained in the DNA so that the organization has the orientation and decision-making skills to move at competitive speed.

3. Establish Plans that Demand Improvements

When a company is winning and at the top of the world, it can be at a vulnerable juncture. It can easily assume that competition will never catch up. It can also fall victim to other assumptions, including the idea that someone else will not exceed existing methodology or technology leadership. We all know these assumptions are not correct, but success has been known to obscure clear thinking.

It is also easy to assume that success will continue because the business has done well in the past, but this may not happen. For instance, a cost basis can easily deteriorate as can market premiums, product life cycles, quality of product and position in the marketplace. No lead will stay if not protected or progressed.

It is for these reasons that, even in the times when the company is delivering strong results and has leadership in the marketplace, aggressive plans need to be pursued. These plans should not be merely financial in nature, but they need to address and improve key activities that cause the improvement in the financial plans. These have to do with obtaining improvements in all the fundamental processes in the business such as quality, manufacturing cycles, new product-development cycles, sales-force productivity, reaching new markets, expanding markets and general levels of productivity in overhead. Particular attention needs to be paid to innovation and creating new markets. Processes have to be robust and have to deliver visibility of how the list of the above factors will improve over the next few years and why.

In essence, you cannot stop running. Continuous, well-planned improvements will provide a good methodology to stay a step ahead.

4. Recognize and Face Up to Structural Changes Early On

For all the above steps the biggest enemy to long-term success is yet to be mentioned in this chapter. These are structural changes that, if not recognized early and tackled aggressively, will fundamentally change the competitiveness of a business or industry. I am not talking about living an alarmist life considering everything as a potential risk; I am talking about significant new factors that, if left unchecked, will serve to erode your business' competitiveness. The process of erosion may take a few years but usually is inexorable.

What are structural changes, how do you detect them early and what do you do about them? Although the list below is not by any means exhaustive, such factors can include a number of the following:

- A new entrant into a marketplace upsetting market behavior and supply; this can be particularly disruptive in a commodity type marketplace

- A new technology or technologies that have been adopted by competitors

- A new technology enabling new entrants from adjacent markets; market destruction from such technologies

- Shifts in patterns of distribution (such as concentration) and shifts in consumer demand or trade preference

- The rise of serious global competitors in emerging markets

- Globalization radically changing economics and competitiveness

- Not participating in rapidly growing markets and thus not developing the skills, products and scale to remain globally competitive in the long term

- Excessive customer or supplier concentration

• Loss of intellectual property protection

• New legislation and regulations

In all these circumstances, how do you detect a problem early and how do you set up your organization to react effectively? The answer to this question leads to the last section of this chapter.

5. Maintain Competitiveness Against Structural Shifts

The first step to avoiding loss of competitiveness in structural shifts is to exhibit daily the right attitude and the avoidance of hubris. Hubris indicates arrogance and overestimation of one's own capabilities and strength. It finds one of its best expressions in Greek tragedy, where the protagonist challenges the laws and the gods (i.e., the factors underlying competitiveness) and this challenge results in his spectacular fall.

The countermeasure to hubris is a culture of robust processes and a senior team that is connected to the marketplace and understands how easily it can lose competitiveness. Time with customers needs to be spent not just by those responsible for customer contact (such as sales, marketing, technical leadership and general management) but also by others who provide services (such as finance, human resources and legal), so they are sensitized to the marketplace. It is essential to keep asking some fundamental questions and to provide regular forums to discuss inherently difficult matters aimed at discovering potential structural shifts.

The quality of these discussions will depend on the amount of time that is dedicated to finding out potential structural shifts and assessing them. Judgment plays the key role. I have seen many situations where a confident team has clearly overestimated its lead and underestimated the capabilities of emerging competitors. Statements such as "They will never get there," or "They do not have the fundamentals in place," or, "It will take them 15 years," can be catastrophic. Guess what? Within three years the competitive landscape has changed radically and what was believed to need 15 years to achieve has already been accomplished. In essence, three years of reaction time and opportunities for countermeasures were lost, usually irretrievably.

The above comments apply very strongly to Chinese competition where the culture, at this time in its history, has all the necessary conditions for breakneck progress: a vast population seeking higher standards of living, low labor costs, export orientation, governmental financial support and people absolutely determined to succeed. Western expectations for comparable achievement and time scales are too generous and too long.

Ultimately, successful leadership is about looking and seeing; it is about exercising the right judgment to arrive at the correct conclusions; and it is about putting in place effective execution. The more people in an organization who can perform these functions at a strategic level, the more assured the success will be. Successful leaders have a clear idea of the factors that make their enterprise successful and systematically strive to stay in touch with them. They also have developed a list of potential threats they need to monitor.

They know what they need to change if the threats materialize. Finally, they have the strong habit of putting all the knowledge together while they look to the future. While accurate forecasting is generally not possible, broad conclusions about the future and competitors are possible. To aid these conclusions, one has to find answers to questions such as:

- If there is a new competitor, where will he or she come from?

- On what basis will the competitor enter the market?

- Under what circumstances would competition have superior economics?

- What technology edge would the competitor need in order to win?

- What geographic or channel strategy would he or she have to take to win?

- What minimum investment and assets would the competitor require and how possible is this?

- Given the change in the environment, are actions we are taking today enabling the success of a competitor in a few years?

All these are classic questions that need to be at the forefront for guidance.

For me, these strategic factors come into sharp focus when I am sitting in front of a customer and have an open-ended discussion about his or her needs, perceptions of my company and perceptions of the competition. Moments like these offer me invaluable information I can gather from no other source. Then, too, meetings with key suppliers, particularly ones with significant technology portfolios, offer valuable perspective, insight and information as well. Devoting a good part of the year to visiting key customers, keeping abreast of developments and looking at everything from a fresh perspective is something a business leader needs to pursue systematically.

On the other hand, leadership cannot be in all places at once and must rely on other people for information while also avoiding overreliance on secondhand information. What people see and what they report has already passed through filters. Continual visits have to be undertaken with eyes wide open by a broad section of the company, not just sales. The objective is to look anxiously over shoulders and discern new trends and threats wherever they may come from. After these have been identified, if judged to be material, there is need for early and decisive action. To counteract a serious structural threat, the action usually will need to be one of magnitude and significant resource commitment, and may also take a long time to be fully implemented.

Ultimately, the test of a successful transformation is whether the organizational DNA and processes have been developed sufficiently to enable continuous capability improvement and to maintain the lead. Given the complex nature of all the factors involved and the continuous balancing act, this will always depend on leadership capability, and, in particular, on leadership judgment.

· · · **Chapter 11 Main Points** · · ·

1. A transformation journey is never entirely complete. After a lead has been established the activity can be less intensive. However, the activity must always continue at a competitive pace, as the lead has to be maintained and protected.

2. Some industries are more forgiving than others, both in terms of the lead required to stay ahead and the ability to recover after falling behind. In high-intensity industries, the journey must be pursued at full intensity on a permanent basis, as an established lead can be lost very quickly.

3. Five steps are recommended to ensure sustainability:

    a) Regularly obtaining and updating common market metrics such as share, customer preference and customer satisfaction. These are a start, but in fast-moving market situations they may already be too past looking in what they show.

    b) Establishing superior performance in areas of industry rhythm and cadence (such as the pace of new product introductions) ensures sustainability and is a strong, long-term predictor of sustainability.

    c) It is imperative to establish plans that constantly demand improvement, even when there is a substantial lead in hand. Particular attention must be paid to innovation and new-market creation.

d) Structural changes in an industry have the potential to destroy any lead established in a transformation. The chapter sets out common situations of major structural shifts and advocates that they need to be recognized early and addressed head on with robust countermeasures.

e) There is need for systematic activity to constantly look out for structural shifts. There is also need to establish regular forums where such developments can be discussed and acted upon. Hubris and assumptions that underestimate what competition can do in these matters must be avoided. The impact of structural shifts can best be seen, and their magnitude best assessed, in discussions with customers. Staying ahead of structural shifts usually requires the early commitment of very substantial resources and the establishment of multiyear programs.

· · · · · · · · ·

Concluding Comments

This book has covered a vast array of related topics. None of these topics is simple, so thank you for staying with it to the end! In fact, even having the road map and guidance provided by the book, adopting the transformation framework set out here it is still an endeavor that will take time and effort. The methodology I have set out is robust but it took me some 30 years of management to develop. Do not expect to get it completely right in the first year. However, do not let the desire for perfection stand in the way of getting started with this outstanding initiative.

Once you start, make the whole process fun, and engage people and enroll their input and excitement. As the leader in the process you may also find your management style is changing, as is your outlook. You might find you have become not only a strong leader but also a strong collaborator, because it is only under these circumstances that people feel free to contribute and work with you.

And now two final comments. First, do not get lost in the detail; know the steps you need to take and follow them systematically. Never let form prevail over substance. Yes, BDW is an integral part of the system and it needs to happen 10 times a year…but does it really need to take the whole week? The answer is no but you need to allow sufficient time to cover comprehensively what you need to. Second, do not fret that you will not develop enough ideas or game-changing moves. Once you begin this systematic way of managing, one idea will lead to another, one discovery will lead to the next, and these findings, coupled with an empowered organization that can speak its mind, will lead you to running the company better than ever with game-changing moves in hand.

—Andreas C. Kramvis

9388073R0

Made in the USA
Charleston, SC
08 September 2011